Chalice of Liberty

Protecting
religious freedom in Australia

CHALICE OF LIBERTY

PROTECTING RELIGIOUS FREEDOM
IN AUSTRALIA

FRANK BRENNAN - M.A. CASEY - GREG CRAVEN

THE KAPUNDA PRESS

(An imprint of Connor Court Publishing)

Series editor DAMIEN FREEMAN

Fellow of the PM Glynn Institute, Australian Catholic University

The Kapunda Press is an initiative of Connor Court Publishing in association with Australian Catholic University's public policy think-tank, the PM Glynn Institute. The Institute is named after one of the Founding Fathers of the Australian Constitution — Patrick McMahon Glynn, who edited the *Kapunda Herald* from 1883 to 1891. This volume is the first to be published under the Kapunda Press imprint, and will be followed by others on matters that speak to the Institute's commitment to generating new approaches and new thinking on public policy issues, and to developing well-supported and practical proposals to address them. These shall include a volume of essays annually in response to the PM Glynn Lecture on Religion, Law and Public Life, the first of which was delivered by the Hon. J. D. Heydon AC QC on 17 October 2017.

Copyright © 2018 as a collection, Damien Freeman; individual chapters, the contributors.

ALL RIGHTS RESERVED. This book contains material protected under International and Federal Copyright Laws and Treaties. Any unauthorised reprint or use of this material is prohibited. No part of this book may be reproduced or transmitted in any form or by any means, electronic or mechanical, including photocopying, recording, or by any information storage and retrieval system without express written permission from the publisher.

CONNOR COURT PUBLISHING PTY LTD

PO Box 7257

Redland Bay QLD 4165

sales@connorcourt.com

www.connorcourt.com

Cover picture: Chalice, mid-17th century, sterling silver gilt 15.3 cm (H), Australian Catholic University Art Collection

ISBN: 9781925501834 (pbk.)

Cover design by Ian James

Printed in Australia

The Kapunda Press
an imprint of Connor Court Publishing
in association with the PM Glynn Institute

Neither the pope in secular matters nor the emperor in spiritual matters has any authority.

Accursius

Contents

Editor's Foreword xi
Damien Freeman

Nine Questions about Religious Freedom 1
Frank Brennan and M. A. Casey

    Democracy, diversity and religious freedom 1
    Why do we need to talk about religious freedom? 4
    What is religious freedom? 10
    What are the limits of religious freedom? 14
    How does religious freedom help build community? 18
    Is religious freedom dangerous for a secular society? 23
    What do Catholics believe about religious freedom today? 29
    What does the law in Australia say about religious freedom? ... 35
    Where do challenges to religious freedom issues in Australia come from? 40
    Is religious freedom discriminatory? 45
    Ten Principles of Religious Freedom 49
    Conclusion 54
    Acknowledgements 55

Protecting Religious Freedom 57
Greg Craven

    What is the human right to freedom of religion? 59

The intersection between freedom of religion and other human rights 71

Australian law's current approach to protecting freedom of religion 77

Is this adequate protection? 82

Recommendations for improving protection of religious freedom 87

Conclusion 96

Endnotes 97

Editor's Foreword

Damien Freeman

In 2016 Australian Catholic University acquired a silver gilt recusant chalice which dates to the seventeenth century. It is of great religious significance, having links back to the English Reformation and the banning of the Mass by Edward VI (1547-53). Recusants refused to comply with this law, despite crushing penalties, and the chalice is described as recusant because it was used in the celebration of illegal Masses. The Vice-Chancellor said, at the time of acquisition, that the chalice was purchased "because it is a living emblem of the centuries of Catholic faith. The chalice represents continuity throughout the period of repression — but also it is a fine example of Catholic traditional art." The chalice connects the University with a period of religious intolerance. As such, it is a reminder of the price that was paid in order to overcome this and to secure religious freedom in England and subsequently Australia.

In the same year, the University established the PM Glynn Institute, as a public policy think-tank to provide the Catholic community with a standing capacity to analyse public policy issues of concern not only to the Catholic Church and its services, but to the wider Australian community as well. The Institute is named in honour of one of the Founding Fathers of the Australian Constitution — Patrick McMahon Glynn, who was not only a barrister and parliamentarian, but also editor of the *Kapunda Herald* from 1883 to 1891. So it is fitting that when the PM

Glynn Institute established its own imprint, in association with Connor Court Publishing, it should be the Kapunda Press.

As the Editor of the Kapunda Press, I am pleased that our first publication addresses the issue of religious freedom. It will be followed by other volumes on matters that speak to the Institute's commitment to generating new approaches and new thinking on public policy issues, and to developing well-supported and practical proposals to address them. The Institute's work is shaped by the proposition that considering the contemporary world in all its complexity also means considering religion and the foundations of faith as important and enduring features of the social and political landscape. So it is also fitting that the Institute's first publication under the Kapunda Press imprint should focus on religious freedom in contemporary Australia.

The purpose of this volume is reflected in its subtitle: protecting religious freedom in Australia. The essay by Fr Frank Brennan SJ and Dr Michael Casey focuses on the first part of this task. It offers some reflections on what exactly religious freedom is and why it is important. It is concerned less with particular issues and how they might be resolved and more with some common concerns or misunderstandings about religious freedom which often haunt discussions about it.

Professor Greg Craven's essay takes up the second part of the task and makes the case for how the law needs to be reformed to enhance protection of religious freedom in Australia. On 22 November 2017, the Prime Minister appointed Philip Ruddock to chair an expert panel charged with examining how freedom of religion is protected in Australia, and recommending how such protection might be improved. The expert panel was required to make its recommendations to the Prime Minister by 31 March 2018. This essay is based on a submission that Professor Craven made to the expert panel.

Religious freedom should be a source of peace, something which deepens hope in the possibility of a world where difference does not always inevitably mean conflict, even if conflict sometimes inevitably remains. This volume was written in pursuit of this hope. May it be shared by all its readers.

Nine Questions about Religious Freedom

Frank Brennan and M.A. Casey

Democracy, diversity and religious freedom

Religious freedom is important to all Australians, not just those of religious faith, because it is a human right which helps make our diverse and democratic society strong. It helps to ensure that diversity is a reality, not just an empty slogan, because it protects the freedom of minorities whose beliefs and practices do not conform to the ruling values and assumptions of the day. It also provides a critical measure of how deeply a society is committed to democratic freedoms. It is a signal of a strong commitment to these freedoms when religious freedom is genuinely valued and generously protected. It is an early warning that not all is well when religious freedom is increasingly treated with suspicion or seen as a problem that needs to be closely constrained.

For believers and non-believers alike, religious freedom is an essential pillar of a strong and decent society, and the purpose of this essay is to show how this is so. Its focus is not primarily on current challenges to religious freedom, although some of these are touched on in the course of the argument. Nor is the paper written as a polemic. Its mode is reflective and discursive, shaped by the hope that in taking some time to wander through the larger landscape in which religious freedom fits, it might just be possible to return to the specific issues of the moment in a different spirit. Meandering through this landscape will not make irreconcilable differences disappear, but it might make it possible to approach them in a spirit of generosity and friendship rather than mistrust and enmity. The possibility of a life in common in a pluralistic and secular society, not just on the issue of religious freedom but on other issues as well, depends on our willingness at least to try this. If we prefer to let our differences make us enemies, a life in common is cast into serious doubt.

The essay is structured around a short series of questions with the intention of clarifying what religious freedom is, what it is not, and why it is important. There is of course much more that could be said on each of these questions and there are some questions which are *not* explored: for example, the different categories of rights, and their foundations and historical development; the role played by mistrust of institutions in general and of Christian churches in particular — especially in light of their failures on issues such as sexual abuse — in generating scepticism about religious freedom; specific issues such as proselytism, and public funding and tax concessions for faith communities; and practical examples of how specific issues, as well as conflicts of rights, might be better resolved. The intention is to provide a high-level discussion for a non-specialist readership of some of the fundamental points for a deeper appreciation of the nature of religious freedom, not a comprehensive account of every facet.

Unsurprisingly for an essay produced by a public policy institute at a Catholic university, it is strongly informed by a Catholic perspective but it is has not been written for Catholics only. Religious freedom is a universal human right, not a special claim for privilege by one denomination or the particular possession of one faith against others. To spell out Catholic appreciation of this essential point, a section of the paper focuses on the Second Vatican Council's landmark declaration on religious freedom, *Dignitatis humanae* (1965). The centrality of respect for freedom in this declaration, specifically the freedom of individuals to seek the truth and to order their lives in light of the truth they find, may surprise readers unfamiliar with Catholic teaching in this area. It is a teaching which has deep roots in the social doctrine of the church. It holds that truth and freedom must go together, and that an act of faith, if it is to be genuine, must be made freely.

Finally, because of the fraught nature of the topic it may be helpful to clarify two points which in other circumstances one might quite comfortably take for granted. First, the views set out in this paper are merely those of the authors and should not be mistaken as representing the views of anyone else (even when, as indicated in a few places, work that the authors have contributed in other places is drawn upon). Secondly, this essay is meant to be a contribution to a conversation that is already well under way. It is by no means the final word.

Why do we need to talk about religious freedom?

Religious freedom occupies a strange place in human rights. It is one of the foundations of democracy and a peaceful, stable society. It is recognised in international treaties as one of a handful of fundamental and inviolable human rights. Yet what it means and what it protects are not well understood, even by those who are religious.

In a secular society like ours it can be easy to overlook what religion contributes to the community, and for people who are not religious it can be difficult to appreciate why faith is so important to individuals. This is one reason why religious freedom is not well understood. Another reason is that for many people, faith is treasured as something very personal and lived out simply each day without encountering much hostility or opposition. Living peacefully in a largely tolerant community like Australia, they do not feel any need to justify their right to believe what they believe or to live the way they live.

Unfortunately this situation is changing. A number of significant challenges to religious freedom have emerged around issues such as the meaning of marriage, the operation of anti-discrimination and anti-vilification laws, and respect for freedom of conscience in healthcare and other professions. These challenges highlight the need to reflect more deeply on what religious freedom means, why it is important, and how it helps to keep a diverse, democratic society strong. This essay is a contribution to this task.

In the first year of his pontificate Pope Francis succinctly summarised the challenge religious freedom faces from strong secularist tendencies in democratic societies today, and how this works against pluralism:

A healthy pluralism, one which genuinely respects differences and values them as such, does not entail privatising religions in an attempt to reduce them to the quiet obscurity of the individual's conscience or to relegate them to the enclosed precincts of churches, synagogues or mosques. This would represent, in effect, a new form of discrimination and authoritarianism. The respect due to the agnostic or non-believing minority should not be arbitrarily imposed in a way that silences the convictions of the believing majority or ignores the wealth of religious traditions. In the long run, this would feed resentment rather than tolerance and peace.[1]

Religious freedom fosters tolerance and peace. It helps to build up a society which genuinely respects and values differences. It works against resentment and conflict. It is a source of resistance to authoritarianism. With other fundamental rights, it should be at the heart of diverse democratic societies, not pushed to the margins.

It is often said that Australia is a very secular country, and on many measures we are. The World Values Survey, for example, found that between 1995 and 2012 the percentage of Australians who said that religion is important in their lives fell from 48 per cent to 31 per cent, while those saying that religion was not at all important to them rose from 19 per cent to 37 per cent. In light of this it is no surprise that over the same period the percentage who said they do not believe in God rose from 19 per cent to 34 per cent. But 64 per cent still reported some level of belief in God in 2012 (down from 75 per cent in 1995).[2]

It was easier in the past than it is today to measure religious life within clear categories. The number of those belonging to the major Christian denominations and the number of regular attenders on Sunday are falling, and the churches as organisations share in the general decline of trust which is affecting all institutions. This is occurring alongside the emergence of new movements within the churches and outside them which are renewing faith and re-energising the service of others.

At the same time, the other great religious traditions of the world have successfully taken root in Australia and are becoming more prominent and important in our community, as the decade between the 2006 and the 2016 censuses highlights. In total, the non-Christian faiths comprised 8.2 per cent of Australians in 2016 (approximately 1.92 million people), compared to 5.6 per cent in 2006 (and 0.7 per cent in 1966). Major traditions such as Hinduism (1.9 per cent or approximately 440,000 people) and Islam (2.6 per cent or approximately 600,000 people) have increased their small number of adherents significantly since the 2006 Census (up from 0.7 and 1.7 per cent respectively). Other traditions such as Sikhism are also growing (from approximately 26,000 people in 2006 to 126,000 in 2016).[3]

A marked change in recent decades has been the increase in the number of those who are not religious at all or do not have any formal religious affiliation. The number of people with "no religion" (30.1 per cent in 2016 — a little over 7 million people — compared to 18.8 per cent in 2006, or 3.7 million people) makes it now the largest single "religious" grouping in the country. One of the most interesting developments underlying these figures is that some who describe themselves as having no religion on the census nevertheless shape their lives around forms of spirituality which combine beliefs and teachings from a range of different traditions in a very personal way.[4]

These changes suggest that it is more accurate to describe contemporary Australia as a pluralist, rather than secular, society, because behind a distinctly secular face, there is an increasingly complex and diverse religious life. We are a country of many religious minorities, and this now includes the different Christian traditions. Although they are usually counted up together to make a majority of the population (52.1 per cent in 2016, compared to 63.9 per cent in 2006), each Christian denomination in itself is a minority (Catholics 22.6 per cent, Anglicans, 13.3 per cent, Uniting Church 3.7 per cent; each falling in their share of the total population from 2006 by 3.2, 5.5 and 2.0 percentage points respectively).[5] This is underscored by the increasing diversity of belief, practice and devotion between the different churches, and even within them, something which is also true of the other faith traditions.

Religion in its many forms is not fading away but growing in importance around the world, and even in Australia. Studies undertaken by the Pew Research Center show that while countries like Australia are becoming more secular, the rest of the world is becoming more religious. The proportion of the global population which is religiously unaffiliated is projected to fall to 12.5 per cent by 2060, down from 16 per cent in 2015. At the same time, Christianity (at 32 per cent) and Islam (at 31 per cent) will together account for nearly two thirds of the world's population (compared to half the global population — 31 per cent and 24 per cent respectively — in 2015). The age profile of religious populations will also be younger than that of unaffiliated or "secular" countries.[6]

Like any human activity, religion can be a force for good or a force for evil. Individuals and organisations motivated by their faith care for some of the most abandoned and oppressed people, draw attention to crimes and injustice which are sometimes overlooked, and work in dangerous situations to bring about peace. At the same time, religious conflict bitterly divides some societies and causes immense destruction.

Religious persecution is one of the major causes of the dramatic increase in the number of refugees. The attempts of some governments and non-government forces to control or suppress different religious communities cause constant suffering and discrimination.[7] Religious minorities are persecuted by governments in many countries, including Sri Lanka and Myanmar for example, and Islamist terrorism is responsible for genocide against ancient religious communities in the Middle East.

Terrorism casts a long shadow of fear and death across many societies, and fear is undoubtedly one reason why the idea of religious freedom is treated with suspicion by some people. In Western countries, fear of religion is predominantly directed against Islam and Muslims. In Australia, where the Muslim community is drawn from many different nations and traditions, fear sometimes obscures how successfully the majority of Muslims have become part of our community.

Other religious traditions are targets not so much of fear as of hatred. The resurgence of anti-Semitism towards the Jewish community in Europe and in some quarters in other Western countries is a reminder of the strength of religious and racial hatred. Christianity too is increasingly a target of hatred, not only for some of its teachings on moral issues such as marriage and sexuality, respect for human life, and human dignity. A worrying increase in the desecration of churches in different countries in Europe suggests that its teachings about its faith are also hated.[8]

In Australia today, thankfully, fear and hatred of different religious traditions and between different religious communities are not the norm, even though there are some tensions and problems can occur. This is an achievement we should not take for granted. We need to keep working to ensure that it continues. Respect for religious freedom helps to make this possible.

It is situations where fear and hatred can come into play, if only at the margins, which remind us most powerfully that human rights are not just for people like ourselves. Human rights are universal, shared by every human being. Among other things, they protect what makes us different from each other. They protect those who think differently, whose beliefs or ideas others find strange, ridiculous or even "offensive", and especially those whom some people hate and fear. Religious freedom is one of these rights.

What is religious freedom?[9]

For most Australians it is a matter of basic fairness for people to be able to put their beliefs into practice and not to be forced to act against them. Religious freedom is a form of this basic fairness. It is not a privilege claimed by religious people for special treatment. It is a fundamental human right, the "manifestation" or exercise of which is, like other fundamental rights, limited by the need to respect the rights of others and the common good.

Religious freedom also means that individuals can practise their religion freely in public, as citizens, and not just in private life. People are entitled to live out their beliefs in co-operation with others who share their faith. Coming together around a common purpose and shared beliefs to build up community and help people in need is the main way in which religious people contribute to strengthening a democratic society.

It is important to appreciate that religious freedom is part of a larger whole. It does not sit in isolation within the concept of human rights but is an integrated and essential part of it. There are three foundational principles of human rights which are particularly important for clarifying this:

- Rights are universal: they belong to each and every human being, and the rights of some individuals or some groups are not more important than the rights of others.
- Rights protect different things which are each important for a fulfilling life. Clearly some rights (e.g. rights protecting people against torture) seem more important than others (e.g. the right to

property). But both protection from torture and the right to property are two fundamental aspects of what respect for human dignity means. Without both we are not really free and we are not able to flourish as we should. Because we need all the different good things which rights protect (life, health, freedom, family, thought, expression, religion, etc.), not just a selection of them, we should approach rights wherever possible as a matter of "both/and", rather than "either/or".

- Rights belong to individuals who live in communities, which can need protection too. For this reason, organisations and institutions are also granted rights, both on their own behalf and as part of the collective exercise of rights and freedoms by individuals (religious schools, for example, assist parents in exercising their freedom to decide the religious and moral education of their children).[10] Because we "should act towards one another in a spirit of brotherhood" (*Universal Declaration of Human Rights*, Article 1), rights should be exercised in solidarity with other people. For this reason the exercise of many rights — whether by individuals alone or collectively, or by organisations — must sometimes be limited to protect the rights and freedom of others.

These principles also apply to religious freedom. To take each one in turn: like other rights, religious freedom is a universal human right. It belongs to every person, whether or not they are religious. Freedom of religion is the right to believe or *not* to believe, to adopt, reject or change beliefs as we decide for ourselves. Partly for this reason it is often called "freedom of religion and belief". Religious freedom arises from our nature as believing creatures.

Consideration of questions of value and meaning seems to be an inescapable part of being human. In searching for answers, no one seems to be satisfied with solutions simply of their own devising. Human beings tend to seek answers to these questions in something greater than themselves.

For many religious people this source of answers will be God, but non-religious people too have ultimate sources — human dignity, justice, freedom, equality, progress, reason, the environment — which affirm their individual sense of life's goodness and the importance of working to make things better. These ultimate sources are in effect revered for the way they go to what is real and true about life, and usually lead to some sense of obligation to live consistently with it. In this sense, questions of meaning and value are religious questions to which we seek religious answers, even if they take the secular forms of atheism or agnosticism.

Because fundamental human rights protect all the things we need to make a full life possible, they have to go together. They should not be placed in opposition to each other or downgraded in importance because some rights — the right to be free from unjust discrimination, for example — are treated as over-riding others.

Understanding different human rights as going together, rather than pulling apart, also highlights the way they make each other possible and reinforce each other. Unless the right to life, for example, is respected, respect for all other rights is placed in doubt, at least to some extent.

In a similar way, respect for freedom of religion and belief both depends on respect for freedom of conscience, freedom of thought, freedom of expression, and freedom of assembly, and supports them in turn. Unless great care is taken, restricting religious freedom unfairly can mean restricting other freedoms as well.

Being free to investigate, reflect, and change our minds, to debate and ask questions, to organise around shared beliefs and concerns, to argue for our views and to try to persuade others, to hold to our convictions about what is right and wrong in the face of pressure or coercion: these things are all essential to the freedom to search for answers to questions of meaning and value.

What are the limits of religious freedom?

Exercising rights in solidarity with other people not only establishes appropriate limits and safeguards, but also provides an important guiding principle for situations where rights come into tension with each other.

Freedom of religion and belief is a fundamental human right, but like many other rights it is not an absolute. One of the most important limits on the exercise of fundamental human rights is respect for the fundamental rights of others. What this means in practice is that we should not assert different rights against each other as some sort of contest where the winner takes all and imposes his or her beliefs on the loser.

For Catholics, the governing principle here was set out in *Dignitatis humanae*, the Second Vatican Council's Declaration on Religious Freedom (1965):

> It is one of the major tenets of Catholic doctrine that man's response to God in faith must be free: no one therefore is to be forced to embrace the Christian faith against his own will. This doctrine is contained in the word of God and it was constantly proclaimed by the Fathers of the Church. The act of faith is of its very nature a free act.[11]

What follows from this is that Catholic beliefs and teachings are not to be imposed on anyone, but proposed for people to accept or reject as they freely decide for themselves. Pope John Paul II underscored this principle in 1990 in speaking of the mission of the church to bring the truth about Jesus Christ to all nations:

> On her part, the Church addresses people with full respect for their freedom. Her mission does not restrict freedom

but rather promotes it. *The Church proposes; she imposes nothing.* She respects individuals and cultures, and she honours the sanctuary of conscience.[12]

This respect for freedom as an essential part of the dignity of the human person lies at the very heart of religious freedom. With it goes respect for the intellect, will and conscience of the individual.[13]

Religious freedom upholds human dignity by protecting people from having the beliefs of others — whether religious, secular or political — imposed on them. This means protecting people from being coerced to act against their beliefs or unjustly prevented from living them out in society. It also protects them against pressure to hide their beliefs or confine them to private life; as well as from being forced to censor themselves or to limit their participation in society to avoid bullying or intimidation.

The other major limit on the exercise of rights comes from the common good,[14] from living in society with other people. Most people appreciate that if we are each to have a significant level of freedom, no one's freedom can be absolute. Laws regulating or limiting rights in appropriate ways aim to give everyone in a democratic society room to move without conflict always arising.

Restrictions to protect public safety and order and which prevent others being endangered or harmed are largely taken for granted as necessary and reasonable. However, important issues arise when restrictions of rights seem to target particular groups who might be of concern to the police or security services, or have the effect of providing only limited protection to vulnerable people such as refugees, or disadvantaged groups such as people living with a disability. There are often important considerations behind restricting rights, but because of the impact it can have on individuals and communities it needs to be approached very carefully.

Less clear and more contested are laws fostering a particular idea of a good society, often supported by people with deep personal commitments to this vision, which limit the rights of some to expand the rights of others. Current examples arise from issues such as: the application of anti-discrimination laws and how they affect religious freedom; the reach of anti-vilification laws and their impact on freedom of speech; laws legalising abortion and euthanasia or assisted suicide and how they restrict freedom of conscience; and the implications of gender theory and same-sex marriage, both of which foreshadow significant limits on each of these rights and some others.

On each of these distinct issues there are divergent views about the extent to which the rights and beliefs of some groups should be advanced at the cost of constraining the rights of others. In different ways they also reflect the expansive vision of individual autonomy which so powerfully shapes our society. Autonomy is a great good and Australians value the high level of personal freedom and independence in our country. The question is how well this is balanced with a strong sense of the common good, of the public consequences or social impacts of private choices we often assert as a right.

Our appreciation of the common good — that often we are best placed to find fulfilment and realise our individual potential by co-operating with others and seeking their good as well — is not as well-developed or as powerful as our appreciation of personal autonomy and our subjective understanding of human rights. This makes the negotiation of the tensions between different rights more fraught. It also contributes to the increasingly acrimonious tone of public discussion of these sorts of issues, which alienates people from each other and hardens hearts and attitudes.

Tensions between rights should be resolved with both the dignity of the person — which includes those who need protection or are unable to speak for themselves, especially children and people who are mentally incapacitated — and the common good in mind. This requires a willingness to find a solution based on mutual respect rather than suspicion. Where there is good faith on all sides, there should be generosity towards beliefs and ways of life we do not share or even oppose. It should also entail a working assumption that solutions which force people to seriously compromise their deepest beliefs will be avoided wherever possible.

How does religious freedom help build community?[15]

People come together with others who share their faith to live out their beliefs. In this way they form communities of believers. Like other groups, most religious communities encourage participation in society, a sense of solidarity with other people, and helping those in need. They also want to maintain their own distinctive culture and beliefs, which helps to enrich society and make diversity a reality rather than a slogan.

Religious communities often generate a range of initiatives to help people and build a good society. For example, the St Vincent de Paul Society (Vinnies) in New South Wales has 387 local conferences, usually parish-based. In 2016-17, a little under 19,000 members and volunteers helped over 60,000 people in their local areas. This included making almost 161,000 visits to people in need — an average of over 400 each day — at their homes, in hospitals and nursing homes, and in support centres and prisons. They provided not only personal support and practical help such as referrals, but also over $17,400,000 in financial assistance, raised from donations.[16]

This sort of contribution to the wider community is not just a social service but a work of religion. The Society's mission is "to live the Gospel message by serving Christ in the poor with love, respect, justice and joy, and by working to shape a more just and compassionate society".[17] In this, it reflects a foundational teaching of the Gospels. In the Gospel of St Mark, Jesus is asked, "Which commandment is first of all?" Jesus answers:

> The first is, "Hear, O Israel: the Lord our God, the Lord is one; you shall love the Lord your God with all your heart,

and with all your soul, and with all your mind, and with all your strength". The second is this, "You shall love your neighbour as yourself". There is no other commandment greater than these. (Mark 12:28-31)

Love of God and love of neighbour are inseparable for Christians, and these two commandments call individual believers to reflect constantly on their own life, the impact they have on those around them, and how they can help others. A similar link between faithfulness to God and helping those around you is a feature of most religious traditions.

The way in which faith and action run together shows that religious belief is never simply a private matter. This reflects a larger reality about human experience. Beliefs and ideas about meaning and truth, right and wrong — religious and non-religious alike — are conclusions about what is real and important in life. Whether they concern how we should live or how things should be in a good society, for all of us they serve as a basis for action in the world.

It is often argued that religious people should quarantine their beliefs from any public activity in which they may be involved, from public debate, and even from the way they carry out their profession or occupation. There are a number of problems with this argument. To begin with, it is simply unfair: it allows everyone to act on their beliefs, except religious people. This sort of unfair treatment is usually called discrimination. The bigger problem with this position, however, is that human life just does not work that way.

No human being lives in neatly divided public and private worlds. In addition to our private lives and our public roles there is the social domain which encompasses both. For example, family life is very personal and private, but it does not end there. It is also social; firstly because it is a group of people who are often living together or otherwise closely connected, and it provides the basis for all sorts of social interactions with other individuals, families and groups. The values and habits which are learnt in the family also have an important social dimension because they help to shape the life of the local community and society more broadly.

Making a rigid distinction between private belief and public action when it comes to the role that religious people play in a democratic society is misleading in two further ways, both for policy making and public understanding. It treats the agencies providing an array of services to society on behalf of religious communities (hospitals, aged care, schools, welfare and other services for vulnerable groups of people) as just another type of non-government or not-for-profit organisation. In doing so, it denies or discounts the importance of the religious beliefs which inspire these works and generate the energy and commitment which make them possible.

It also reflects a failure to take faith seriously. It treats religious belief as nothing more than a form of subjective or personal opinion, with no real significance beyond the individual who holds it. No one has to like religion or even be interested in it, but placing it wishfully on the same level as a personal interest or superstition is not helpful to a full understanding of the world in which we live.

Faith so powerfully informs the way believers live, the actions they take, and the shape of communities because it is a matter of considered and deeply-held conviction. As a result, it brings many good things with it. Like other forms of conviction

— philosophical, ideological, political, economic, moral — religious convictions can also be wrong or unjust, and they can lead to oppression or destruction. Dealing with this reality, however, is not helped by misunderstanding what religion is.

The right to freedom of religion and belief is a fundamental human right because of religion's importance to people as a matter of deep conviction. This is why it protects not only the freedom of religious people to pray and worship, but also the freedom to live out their beliefs in the services they provide for the wider community, and to operate these services in accordance with their beliefs. It also protects the right to publicly explain their beliefs and to propose them for the acceptance of others.

Religious freedom is sometimes spoken of as if it means little more than freedom of worship, with faith-based services to the wider community excluded from its protection. This has the effect of reducing it to something like a narrow concept of toleration for minorities with strange opinions. In part, this reflects the incomprehension of some about what religion is. In part, it reflects the hostility of others to religion in itself. It also reflects a lack of curiosity and interest in those who are different from us, which does not help to strengthen a diverse society.

In the face of this incomprehension and hostility, religious freedom protects not only the right of individuals and religious communities to fully participate in the life of a democratic society, but also the contribution they make to building it up. This means protecting their freedom to live out their beliefs in the public and social domains, as local volunteers and in their agencies and services, respecting always the rights and freedoms of others.

On his visit to the United States in September 2015, Pope Francis met with Hispanic Americans and other migrant groups to speak to them about religious freedom and captured these ideas very succinctly:

> Religious freedom certainly means the right to worship God, individually and in community, as our consciences dictate. But religious liberty, by its nature, transcends places of worship and the private sphere of individuals and families. Because religion itself, the religious dimension, is not a subculture; it is part of the culture of every people and every nation.[18]

Is religious freedom dangerous for a secular society?

Religious believers in Australia are citizens who have the same rights and responsibilities as everyone else to take part in public debate and to participate in politics. Religious leaders are also entitled to contribute to public discussion, and in doing so carry out an important responsibility to their communities and to society as a whole.

For Catholics, participation in politics and the public square is primarily the vocation of lay people rather than bishops and priests, who can also contribute to this work in different ways. It can take many forms including leading agencies or works sponsored by different parts of the church, taking the initiative to form independent groups and associations to address important issues or needs, and individual involvement in a range of political and social groups.

Whenever people from different faith traditions take part in public discussions, particularly on contentious issues, there are some who try to exclude or discredit their contribution by claiming that "religious" views have no place in debates about "secular" matters. Underlying this claim sometimes is an assertion that religious arguments are inherently irrational while secular arguments are all about "reason". Typically this claim arises when the concerns that religious people raise — whether about euthanasia, same-sex marriage, refugees and asylum seekers, or the poor and unemployed — inconveniently highlight issues which some would prefer not to discuss.

There are two common public arguments in favour of restricting religious freedom. The first is that religion is a potential source of conflict and division in society. The second is that religious people want to impose their beliefs on others, and given the opportunity, will try to use the law and government to do so. Both these concerns treat religion as a threat to the fundamental rights and freedoms of others, which puts religious freedom in an unusual category as a "dangerous" human right which can only be allowed with great caution. The impact of Islamist terrorism has deepened this view and helped to generate greater support for restrictions on the exercise of religious freedom more generally.

Looking at Australia over the last fifty or sixty years, however, the concern that religious belief and diversity are potential sources of conflict is not supported by the historical record. A dramatic rise in the religious diversity of the country has been accompanied by a steep decline in the sectarian differences between Christians which featured significantly in our history up to the middle of the twentieth century.

More recently, there have been tensions in relations with newer ethnic and religious groups, particularly in the context of concerns about terrorism and security. For the most part, however, different religions in Australia usually combine devotion to their own beliefs and traditions with respect for other faiths, often accompanied with a willingness to establish good relations and some level of co-operation. A shared commitment to the rule of law, to equality under the law, and to applying the law consistently to everyone in our community, are essential elements in maintaining this situation.

Religious freedom is not the problem in situations of tension, but part of the solution. Pope Francis has observed that religious freedom is:

a fundamental right which shapes the way we interact socially and personally with our neighbours whose religious views differ from our own. The ideal of inter-religious dialogue, where all men and women, from different religious traditions, can speak to one another without arguing. This is what religious freedom allows.[19]

History is of course replete with examples of religion becoming entangled with political power, and the world today provides more examples. The Catholic Church has not been immune to this at different times. In earlier centuries this was sometimes because of feudal and dynastic reasons and assumptions about the role of the church in a specifically Christian society. At the local level in different places, this has sometimes occurred because of issues around political patronage and property.

In other situations the church acquired political power or influence because of the way in which it became a means for a community under the domination of other powers to express and preserve its distinct cultural and national identity — Ireland, Quebec and Poland are three examples. Situations can still arise in the developing world today (as they did in ancient times during the collapse of the Roman empire) when government breaks down, especially during natural disasters or civil war, and bishops or other church leaders have to effectively become civil administrators to ensure that people are helped and protected.

One of the most important safeguards against the inappropriate involvement of religion in politics is the separation of church and state. This tends to be understood today primarily as a principle which protects the state and society against the encroachments of religion. There is an assumption in this that religion is in some way a threat to democratic society that has to be guarded against. In reality, however, this principle was first conceived to protect faith communities from being dominated or controlled by government. The separation of church and state is meant to ensure the independence of both.

We take for granted the freedoms and opportunities of modern, democratic, secular societies today, forgetting how utterly different they are from societies across most of human history. In those societies, religion and political authority were not separated but bound closely together. One of the reasons Christians were persecuted in the Roman empire prior to Constantine was that they refused to worship the Roman gods. Religion was used to legitimise political authority, so refusing to offer sacrifice to the gods not only made Christians impious but a threat to the stability of society.

Separating church and state, religion and politics, has been one of the major currents of Western history, and its origins lie in the efforts of the early church to secure its independence from political rulers in matters of faith, as well as in arranging its own internal affairs. This struggle began with the conversion of Constantine, which put an end to the persecution of Christians but brought with it the Emperor's intense interest in theological questions and the appointment of bishops. It led in time to the first clear formulation of the separation of "church and empire" as a principle, which was provided not by a thinker of the Enlightenment but by Pope Gelasius I in the fifth century.[20]

A major foundation of the separation of church and state in the West comes from the Gospels, especially from Jesus' teaching to "render unto Caesar the things that are Caesar's, and to God the things that are God's" (Luke 20:20-26). More radically still, as Pope Benedict XVI has argued, the universality of Jesus' teaching broke with the assumptions of his time that religion must be embodied in politics and society; that a particular faith requires a particular social order as the only legitimate way of arranging life in common.[21]

As Pope Benedict has observed (with others before him), "the Sermon on the Mount [Matthew 5-7] cannot serve as the foundation for a state and a social order .... Its message seems to be located on another level." Ultimately, the consequence of this was that "concrete juridical and social forms and political arrangements [could] no longer be treated as sacred law". The absence of social and political prescriptions in the teaching of Jesus released the political and social order "from the directly sacred realm, from theocratic legislation". It allowed different societies to work out their own arrangements for their time and place in the light of his message, because this message is universal and not bound to any particular time or place or people.[22]

Religions can be tempted by political power, but political power can also be tempted by the authority of religion or the aura of the sacred, which can very easily attach to apparently secular purposes, as the history of the twentieth century shows.[23] The separation of church and state is one protection against this. The life of faith lived well is another, as Pope Francis reminds us:

> Our various religious traditions serve society primarily by the message they proclaim. They call individuals and communities to worship God, the source of all life, liberty and happiness. They remind us of the transcendent dimension of human existence and our irreducible freedom

in the face of any claim to absolute power .... They call to conversion, reconciliation, concern for the future of society, self-sacrifice in the service of the common good, and compassion for those in need. At the heart of their spiritual mission is the proclamation of the truth and dignity of the human person and all human rights.[24]

What do Catholics believe about religious freedom today?[25]

The Catholic understanding of religious freedom changed significantly with the Second Vatican Council (1962-65). This occurred through the working out of the principles of Catholic social teaching elaborated by Pope Leo XIII in the last decades of the nineteenth century; and through the recovery of foundational Christian understandings about both the appropriate roles of government and the church, and the centrality of freedom to an act of faith.[26]

Leading up to the Council, the approach of the Catholic Church to religious freedom was reflected in the work of the Theological Commission which was preparing preliminary documents for the Council. The Commission saw the need for the Council to consider the question of church-state relations.

The Commission took the view (not uncommon among Catholics at that time) that if most citizens of the state were Catholic, the state too had a duty to profess Catholicism. Those few citizens of other faiths were not seen as having the right to profess their religions, although the state might tolerate them for the common good. In countries where the majority were non-Catholic, the church argued that Catholics had the right to be completely free to profess their faith and the church should be free to undertake its mission.

International understanding of religious freedom had developed significantly in the years after the Second World War. In 1948 the World Council of Churches at its first assembly in Amsterdam published a declaration on religious liberty. Declaring that "an essential element in a good international order is freedom of religion", the WCC specified four rights including: "every person has the right to determine his own faith and creed"; and "every person has the right to express his religious beliefs in worship, teaching and practice, and to proclaim the implications of his beliefs and relationships in a social or political community".

Four months later the General Assembly of the United Nations approved the *United Nations Declaration of Human Rights* recognising "the inherent dignity and the equal and inalienable rights of all members of the human family". Article 18 provides:

> Everyone has the right to freedom of thought, conscience and religion; this right includes freedom to change his religion or belief, and freedom, either alone or in community with others and in public or private, to manifest his religion or belief in teaching, practice, worship and observance.

Pope John XXIII recognised the need for the church's approach in this area to develop so as to better respond to new social and political circumstances. A major resource for this task was the social teaching of the church, particularly Pope Leo XIII's encyclical *Rerum novarum* (1891), and Pope Pius XI's encyclical *Quadragesimo anno* (1931), both of which articulated a compelling defence of the rights of individuals and families against the power of the state and the unregulated economy.[27]

Drawing on this tradition and developing it further, in 1963 John XXIII outlined the church's commitment to human rights in his encyclical *Pacem in terris*, writing that:

> Any well-regulated and productive association of men

in society demands the acceptance of one fundamental principle: that each individual man is truly a person. His is a nature, that is, endowed with intelligence and free will. As such he has rights and duties, which together flow as a direct consequence from his nature. These rights and duties are universal and inviolable, and therefore altogether inalienable.

One of those rights was "that of being able to worship God in accordance with the right dictates of his own conscience, and to profess his religion both in private and in public".[28]

In 1965, Pope Paul VI promulgated *Dignitatis humanae,* the Council's Declaration on Religious Freedom. The document had gone through six complete redrafts before agreement was reached by the bishops. One of the principal authors of the declaration, Fr John Courtney Murray SJ, saw work on the declaration as an urgent matter for the Council. He was concerned that the Catholic Church was late in bringing its authority to the question in a situation where, despite continuing violations of religious freedom in the world, "the principle itself is accepted by the common consciousness of men and civilised nations".[29]

One of the issues confronting the Council was how to acknowledge the right to religious freedom without it being confused with secular ideas of individual freedom and autonomy released from any notion of objective truth; what we would describe today as moral relativism.

Dignitatis humanae addresses this problem by making it clear that "the right to religious freedom has its foundation in the very dignity of the human person as this dignity is known through the revealed word of God and by reason itself". As human beings, "that is, beings endowed with reason and free will and therefore privileged to bear personal responsibility", we have "a moral obligation to seek the truth, especially religious truth", and once it has been found, to live out our lives "in accord with the demands of truth".[30]

Fulfilling this obligation to seek out the truth requires freedom, which means both "immunity from external coercion as well as psychological freedom". This freedom belongs to everyone, even "those who do not live up to their obligation of seeking the truth and adhering to it".[31] It is an obligation which cannot be enforced, because it falls "upon the human conscience". "As the truth is discovered, it is by a personal assent that men are to adhere to it".[32]

It is for all these reasons that the Council could declare that:

> The human person has a right to religious freedom. This freedom means that all persons are to be immune from coercion on the part of individuals or of social groups and of any human power, [in such a way] that no one is to be forced to act in a manner contrary to their own beliefs, whether privately or publicly, whether alone or in association with others, within due limits.[33]

Because we are social creatures, religious freedom also means the freedom to give external expression to one's faith, to "share with others in matters religious" and to profess one's "religion in community". Governments should take the religious life of its citizens seriously "and show it favour, since the function of government is to make provision for the common welfare". [34]

While governments should not use their power to "command or inhibit acts that are religious",[35] "due limits" means that those exercising religious freedom have to pay appropriate regard to the common good. The Council acknowledged this repeatedly in *Dignitatis humanae*. Observing and accepting "the just demands of public order" is one of the duties that goes with religious freedom. In maintaining public order, governments can constrain the exercise of freedom of religion to protect the rights of all citizens, to maintain the public peace, and to preserve public morality. In doing so, however, governments must not act in an arbitrary or unfair or partisan manner.[36]

Dignitatis humanae teaches that religious freedom as a right arises not only from respect for the dignity of the person and respect for a person's freedom, but from the duty that each person has to "seek the truth ... and to hold fast to it". However, the powerful influence of moral relativism today makes it difficult to understand religious freedom and freedom of conscience as much more than a right to have our own personal passions and commitments "respected".

The "solution" democratic societies deploy to deal with the diversity of passions and commitments in a modern society, particularly in the matters of religion and conscience, is to treat them as being only subjectively important to the people who hold them. What this means practically is that they have to be confined to the private domain so that they do not intrude into public or professional life. At a time when people are disenchanted, disengaging, and increasingly divided, this is unlikely to be sustainable, for the simple reason that it trivialises what is most important to people.

Reflecting on the nature of life, our responsibilities to others, and what helps to make for a good society can bring people to inconvenient conclusions. Relativising and privatising these conclusions effectively excludes them from public discussion as if they were simply irrational or bigoted. This helps to impose an "official" view about certain subjects on public life and our life in common, and makes for intolerance of different perspectives, rather than mutual respect. As political developments in recent years have shown, people are increasingly unwilling to accept official views on many things.

Counter-intuitively perhaps, religious freedom actually encourages both a sense of common purpose and a spirit of friendship, because it reminds us that we are united in a search for truth, even if the conclusions we reach are radically opposed to each other. Living together in this shared search requires listening, engagement and being able to disagree without hatred, not silencing and exclusion. As we speak to each other about our different convictions, we need to keep in mind that "the truth cannot impose itself except by virtue of its own truth, as it makes its entrance into the mind at once quietly and with power".[37] Imposing "truth" on other people calls its claim to be the truth into serious doubt.

What does the law in Australia say about religious freedom?[38]

A year after the Vatican Council concluded, the United Nations finalised the *International Covenant on Civil and Political Rights* (ICCPR), which brings greater specificity to the right of freedom of religion than in the original 1948 *United Nations Declaration of Human Rights*.[39] Australia is a signatory to this convention and it plays an important part in human rights law in our country.

It is a reflection of how cherished the right to religious freedom is in international law that under the Covenant it cannot be suspended or limited in times of national emergency. Most rights under the ICCPR — including rights we usually think of as essential to a democracy such as freedom of speech, freedom of association, equality before the law and the right to privacy — can be limited (or "derogated") to the extent strictly required by the demands of the situation "in time of public emergency which threatens the life of the nation". This is not the case for freedom of religion. Along with rights such as the right to life, protections against torture and slavery, and the right to be recognised as a person before the law, it is "non-derogable".[40]

Australia signed the ICCPR in 1972, which came into force when it was formally adopted by the international community in 1976. The convention began to play a role in Australian law in 1980, but our commitment to religious freedom has a much longer history. It was a subject of debate and discussion in the Constitutional Conventions which led to Federation and an Australian Constitution. Speaking to the 1897 Constitutional Convention, the future Prime Minister Edmund Barton expressed the prevailing view about the separation of church and state, and freedom of religion:

> The whole mode of government, the whole province of the State, is secular. ... The whole duty is to render unto Caesar the things that are Caesar's, and unto God the things that are God's. That is the line of division maintained in every State in which there is not a predominant church government which dictates to all civil institutions.[41]

It is instructive that the delegates to the Convention did not think it was inconsistent with the separation of church and state to include an acknowledgement of God in the Constitution itself. Thanks to the efforts of another Convention delegate, Patrick McMahon Glynn, the Australian Constitution, as approved by the Australian people and enacted by the Imperial Parliament, set out in its preamble that the people were "humbly relying upon the blessing of Almighty God" in uniting "in one indissoluble Federal Commonwealth under the Crown".

The Australian Constitution also makes a specific provision for religious freedom in section 116:

> The Commonwealth shall not make any law for establishing any religion, or for imposing any religious observance, or for prohibiting the free exercise of any religion, and no religious test shall be required as a qualification for any office or public trust under the Commonwealth.

This provision echoes some of the language of the First Amendment of the Constitution of the United States, but it has been interpreted and applied much less expansively, reflecting the different histories of the two countries and their different approaches to constitutional law.

Section 116 includes four prohibitions, but those prohibitions apply to the Commonwealth and not to the States. The Commonwealth is prohibited from making laws which interfere with freedom of religion, but that prohibition might not extend to all other Commonwealth activities. The constitutional limitation on Commonwealth legislative power relates to the "establishment", "observance", "free exercise" and any "religious test". Even though the constitutional guarantee limits the power of the Commonwealth in this area, it does not explicitly create a personal or individual right to religious freedom.

Another important question concerns what constitutes a religion under Australian law. The High Court of Australia has given a broad reading to the concept of religion. In 1983, ruling on the application of the Church of the New Faith (the Church of Scientology) for charitable tax exemptions on the basis that it qualified as a religion, High Court judges identified various characteristics for recognising a set of beliefs and practices as a religion.[42]

Two of the justices (Acting Chief Justice Mason and Justice Brennan) highlighted two criteria; "first, belief in a supernatural Being, Thing or Principle; and second, the acceptance of canons of conduct in order to give effect to that belief", emphasising that "canons of conduct which offend against the ordinary laws are outside the area of any immunity, privilege or right conferred on the grounds of religion".[43]

Two other justices (Justices Wilson and Deane) set out five elements which define a religion. Firstly, a set of ideas and practices is unlikely to be a religion unless it "involves belief in the supernatural, that is to say, belief that reality extends beyond that which is capable of perception by the senses".

Following from this, it must: "relate to man's nature and place in the universe and his relation to things supernatural"; and be "accepted by adherents as requiring or encouraging them to observe particular standards or codes of conduct or to participate in specific practices having supernatural significance". The final elements are that "however loosely knit and varying in beliefs and practices adherents may be, they constitute an identifiable group or identifiable groups", and "that the adherents themselves see the collection of ideas and/or practices as constituting a religion".[44]

The Australian Law Reform Commission (ALRC) thinks these definitions are wide enough to apply to most religions, "but may raise questions about their application to, for example, Buddhism or indigenous religion or spirituality".[45]

The law's attempts to define the major features of a religion underscore that religious freedom is not a claim for special privilege by a particular religious community such as the Catholic Church. It is a right which belongs to everyone. This means it must be accorded to all other faiths and religious organisations, no matter how small they are or how strange or novel their beliefs and practices might seem to be to others.

Respecting freedom of religion and belief does not mean treating every conviction as equally valid, or that every exercise or manifestation or belief is equally permitted. The ALRC notes the important distinction between the right to adopt a religion or system of belief as one chooses for oneself, which is unlimited, and the exercise or manifestation of that religion or belief, which can be limited to protect public safety and order or the rights of others:

Clearly, the right to manifest religion or belief 'does not always guarantee the right to behave in public in a manner governed by that belief'. That is, once a belief is 'manifested (that is, implemented) in action, it leaves the sphere of absolute protection, because the manifestation of a religious belief may have an impact on others'.[46]

Restrictions on the exercise of religious freedom must be made on a principled basis that applies to all religions, in particular the responsibility to protect the fundamental rights and freedoms of other people. Whenever people might be prepared to countenance restrictions on the religious practices of small religious groups or major religious traditions, it should be on the basis that the same principles apply to everybody.

Where do challenges to religious freedom issues in Australia come from?

In many places in the world today religious freedom is a matter of life and death. At a time of rising religious persecution and conflict, which has seen people killed and enslaved because of their faith, houses of worship attacked and destroyed, different communities targeted by mob violence or terrorism, and a massive increase in the number of refugees and displaced people, Australia remains a place of immense safety and freedom for members of all religious traditions.

Whatever challenges confront religious freedom in Australia, persecution is not among them. There is no denial of freedom to worship and people are free to choose or change their religion, or to have no religion at all. Our laws do not protect religious beliefs or communities from scrutiny and debate, or punish people solely because they criticise them (although the operation of anti-vilification laws in some circumstances could change this). All of this is good, and it is important to keep it in mind when considering the very different sorts of challenges that religious freedom faces in a democratic society.

Nonetheless, there are issues which pose serious challenges for religious communities in Australia. Some of the most important to date have arisen in areas such as relationships and sexuality, and respect for life at its beginning and end in healthcare. In other Western countries religious freedom issues have also arisen in the area of social justice, when laws targeting vulnerable groups such as illegal immigrants have attempted to prohibit religious groups from providing them with assistance, including sacramental and pastoral support.[47] So far, this is not the case in Australia.

Questions concerning relationships and sexuality, beginning of life issues such as abortion and particular reproductive technologies, and end of life issues such as euthanasia and assisted suicide, are quite distinct from each other. They are complex and multi-faceted and engage many deeply felt concerns on all sides. A common thread running through each issue however, is a powerful idea of autonomy which has its origins in the commitment of democratic societies to the dignity of the person and respect for each individual's freedom.

Across these quite different issues, the commitment to autonomy seems to work itself out in a similar way. It leads to an insistence that certain preferred positions on these questions are the only ones available to people who are genuinely committed to justice and fairness. Those who do not agree with these preferred positions because they are motivated by different convictions about justice and fairness are characterised as discriminatory, bigoted or judgemental, or as wishing to impose their own values on other people.

One of the implications of this approach is that allowing people to act on such different convictions is treated as a threat to the autonomy of others. This is seen as something which cannot be tolerated in a decent society. It is also asserted that permitting some people to withhold endorsement of some preferred position and to act on this in their public or professional activity "disrespects" or disparages the choices of those with whom they disagree.[48]

Forcing debate about these important issues into such an exclusionary or restrictive framework makes conflict inevitable, because it refuses to allow room to disagree. One example is the issue of legal recognition of same-sex relationships, whether through anti-discrimination and equality laws, bills of rights, civil unions or same-sex marriage. This has been accompanied in different Western countries by a strong tendency to mandate public endorsement of new concepts of marriage, family and sexuality, and punish those who are unable to comply.

Examples from overseas include: closing down church-run adoption and fostering services which, because of their beliefs about marriage, family and the best interests of the child, are unable to place children with same-sex couples,[49] increasing pressure to restrict what religious schools can teach about marriage, family, and sexuality if it runs counter to the new understanding,[50] requiring civil marriage celebrants and registrars to assist at same-sex marriages and civil unions despite their religious or conscientious objections,[51] and penalising people who do not believe in same-sex marriage, even to the point of forcing them out of their jobs or businesses.[52]

Healthcare is another area where, to protect autonomy as a supreme value, dissent on some controversial issues is increasingly not tolerated. The Victorian *Abortion Law Reform Act* provides an example of the restrictions placed on health practitioners' right to conscientious objection. It requires practitioners with a conscientious objection (which may or may not be a religious objection) to assist women seeking an abortion by referring them to another practitioner who is willing to perform this procedure.[53] In effect, this leaves many health practitioners in the situation where following their conscience can breach the law.

Medical professionals should be allowed to act according to their deeply held convictions and beliefs, consistent with the right to conscientious objection protected by the *United*

Nations Declaration of Human Rights and in the ICCPR, and recognised in international and national codes of professional ethics.[54] The law in Australia should uphold the right of a doctor to conscientiously object to carrying out or referring for an abortion without any personal or professional disadvantage.

The sorts of considerations about freedom of conscience and religion that apply to abortion also apply to the legalisation of euthanasia or assisted suicide. Doctors and other healthcare professionals should not be forced to participate in this against their conscience and neither should they be expected to provide a referral to another medical practitioner, either for the administration of a lethal injection or for a prescription for self-administered lethal medication, should they have a conscientious objection to participating in any way in such a procedure.[55]

The rights of religious communities which provide aged care and end-of-life care must also be respected. In some countries, Christian aged care facilities have been penalised by courts and governments for refusing to allow assisted suicide or euthanasia to be performed on their premises.[56] Individuals with conscientious or religious objections to abortion have been ordered to assist in the procedure, and threatened with being excluded from studying for or practising their professions in healthcare if they refuse to comply.[57]

The growing intolerance towards the right to conscientious objection in healthcare is reflected in a statement developed by a group of influential bioethicists meeting at the Brocher Foundation in Switzerland in June 2016. The statement describes conscientious objection to abortion or "medical assistance in dying" as "indefensible". It calls for conscientious objectors to be examined before tribunals for sincerity and "reasonability", and "to compensate society and the health system for their failure to fulfil their professional obligations". It also calls for medical students to learn "how to perform basic medical procedures they consider to be morally wrong", because they should be required to perform these procedures in "emergency situations".[58]

This example highlights an important feature common to all the issues discussed in this section: much of the energy driving many of the challenges to religious freedom and conscientious objection comes from within the community. Historically, human rights were seen as a protection first and foremost against the power of the state. Today, while significant challenges arise from laws and government regulations and policies, a hardness of feeling against these rights is also clearly apparent among various non-government organisations, some community and activist groups, and the attitudes expressed over social media. When these different voices come together to advance a particular issue or to discourage dissenting voices, it is not unusual for those who disagree to experience something which feels like intimidation.

This situation provides another reason for being clear about what religious freedom is and why it is important. Religious freedom and conscientious objection protect people from being compelled to endorse or co-operate with activates which they consider, as a matter of conviction, to be wrong. Conscientious objection in particular can be the last protection of very vulnerable people. In other times and places these rights have allowed people to speak out against injustice and evil when no one else will. Restricting these rights unfairly is not simply a matter of restricting the freedom of religious organisations or isolated individuals. It also deprives society of a voice of conscience.

Is religious freedom discriminatory?[59]

A particular area of concern for religious freedom in Australia is the interpretation and impact of anti-discrimination laws. Most of these laws at state and federal level include "exemptions" or "exceptions" for religious communities (and other communities for various purposes) so that they can administer their own affairs and run their schools and services in ways which are consistent with their beliefs. In this way, exemptions are a form of protection for religious freedom, although the word "exemption" tends to suggest a special privilege which exempts a religious community from the laws which apply to everyone else. Acknowledging this problem, the Australian Law Reform Commission has suggested giving further consideration "to whether freedom of religion should be protected through a general limitations clause rather than exemptions".[60]

A particular focus concerns whether, in employing people, religious bodies are entitled to exercise a preference for those who are actively committed to their mission, and if so, how far this preference can extend. In the setting of a religious school, a legislative approach which focuses on the "inherent requirements" of a role could significantly restrict the circumstances in which a religious employer could require staff to support the mission of the service. It might be argued that the principal and the religion teachers need to support the mission as an inherent requirement of their role, but not support staff or teachers in other subject areas in the school.

In practice today, the concern here is not so much about being able to employ *only* those who share a particular faith in a religious agency or service, but having the freedom to ensure that a least a critical mass among the staff share this commitment and witness to it in their work and lives. There is also strong concern that an inherent requirement test in anti-discrimination laws could force faith-based schools and organisations to hire staff who do not support — or who even oppose — the religious community's beliefs and mission.

As Cardinal Pell has pointed out, "church agencies and schools are not exempt from anti-discrimination law". At the same time, "parliaments are obliged by international human rights conventions like the ICCPR to provide protection of religious freedom in any laws which would unfairly restrict the right of religious communities to operate their schools and services in accord with their beliefs and teachings". The argument is about treating religious groups like others in the community:

> Should the Greens have the right to prefer to employ people who believe in climate change, or should they be forced to employ sceptics? Should Amnesty International have the right to prefer members who are committed to human rights, or should they be forced to accept those who admire dictatorships? Both cases involve discrimination and limiting the freedoms of others, and without it neither organisation would be able to maintain their identity or do their job effectively.[61]

In their submission to a federal government inquiry into consolidating anti-discrimination law in 2012, Professors Patrick Parkinson and Nicholas Aroney observed that:

> Great care needs to be taken to ensure that a focus on the first-mentioned right (freedom from discrimination) does not diminish the others (e.g. freedom of religion, association and cultural expression and practice). This

can readily happen, for example, if freedom of religion is respected only grudgingly and at the margins of anti-discrimination law as a concessionary 'exception' to general prohibitions on discrimination. It can also happen if inadequate attention is paid to freedom of association and the rights of groups to celebrate and practise their faith and culture together.[62]

These dangers are real. Some advocates for reform of anti-discrimination laws have a tendency to place a very high value on "non-discrimination" and to concede "exceptions" based upon freedom of religion, association or cultural expression only with great reluctance, if at all. Although they sometimes recognise that there is a need to give due weight to all human rights, it is generally not acknowledged that posing the question as one of identifying exceptions to the principle of non-discrimination prejudices the inquiry in its favour. The practical result is that the rights to freedom of religion, association and culture, are treated as rights of lesser importance.

Clear protections for religious freedom — described as protections, rather than exemptions which have to be proven to apply — are required so that faith communities can witness to their faith with integrity. At the same time, Catholic institutions must also be faithful to their commitment to respecting the dignity and freedom of every person. For example, it is not necessarily hostility which might lead some people to conclude that Catholic schools would be contradicting their own beliefs if people involved in same-sex relationships were excluded from employment in key positions, while heterosexual people in relationships which also do not reflect Catholic teaching still qualified. The same principles should apply to everyone.

When these issues arise within Catholic agencies and services, the emphasis should always be on seeking a pastoral resolution wherever possible, which respects the rights and dignity of all concerned. This approach should be applied more generally in the community, resetting the defaults from suspicion to a spirit of generosity, friendship and trust which accepts differences and does not require people on either side to compromise their deeply held convictions.

In *Dignitatis humanae*, the Vatican Council stated: "government is to see to it that equality of citizens before the law, which is itself an element of the common good, is never violated, whether openly or covertly, for religious reasons. Nor is there to be discrimination among citizens".[63] As John Courtney Murray commented in his published notes to the Declaration, "this statement about equality before the law as an element of the common welfare has an accent of newness in official Catholic statements. It is important for the construction of the full argument of religious freedom".[64]

Ten Principles of Religious Freedom

The reflections on the different aspects of freedom of religion and belief which have been offered in this essay can be set out as a series of principles. They start from the fact that religious belief is a considered and deeply-held conviction which powerfully informs the way believers live, the actions they take, and the shape of communities. It is not just another form of subjective or personal opinion significant only for the individual who holds it. Religious freedom arises from the universal human search for the truth about our nature, the world we live in, and how we should live.

1. Freedom of religion and belief is a universal human right

Religious freedom belongs to every person, because most people look for answers to questions of meaning and value in something greater than themselves. Many religious people look to God, but non-religious people also draw on ultimate sources of meaning which are not of their making, such as ideas about human dignity, justice, freedom, equality, and the environment. In one sense, questions of meaning and value are religious questions even when our answers are atheism or agnosticism.

2. Religious freedom is based on respect for individual freedom

"The act of faith is of its very nature a free act" (*Dignitatis humanae* §10). Religious freedom is the right to believe or *not* to believe, to adopt, reject or change beliefs as we decide for ourselves. It protects freedom by protecting people from having the beliefs of others —religious, secular or political — imposed on them. Catholic beliefs too are not to be imposed on anyone, but proposed for people to accept or reject as they decide freely for themselves.

3. Religious freedom protects human dignity

Religious freedom upholds the intrinsic dignity of people who think, believe, worship and live differently. It protects them against pressure to hide their beliefs, or from being forced to censor themselves or limit their participation in society to avoid bullying or intimidation. It defends them from discrimination, exclusion or punishment because of their beliefs. Religious freedom is especially important in protecting people whose beliefs or ideas others find strange, ridiculous or even "offensive", and particularly communities which may be hated and feared because of their beliefs.

4. Religious freedom should be exercised in solidarity with other people

Like many rights, religious freedom is not an absolute. It is limited by respect for both the rights of others and the common good. Because our sense of autonomy is often stronger than our sense of the common good, agreeing on the limits of rights can be fraught. Tensions between rights should be resolved wherever possible in a spirit of mutual respect, not suspicion, and with generosity towards beliefs and ways of life we do not share or even oppose. Restrictions on religious freedom should be made only on the basis of principles which apply to everyone.

5. Religious freedom is more than freedom of worship or a right to tolerance

The persecution of people in different parts of the world because of their religious beliefs shows how important basic protections such as freedom to worship and the right to be tolerated are, but religious freedom does not end there. It is a much larger freedom which makes it possible for individuals and faith communities to witness to their beliefs with integrity and as full members of their society, not only in worship but in professional life, public life and service to the wider community.

6. Religious freedom allows individuals to practise their religion freely and publicly as citizens, and not just in private life

The claim that religious people should quarantine their beliefs from public debate and even from the way they carry out their profession or occupation is unfair and discriminatory, because it allows everyone except religious people to act on their beliefs. No human being lives in neatly divided public and private worlds. Beliefs about meaning and truth, right and wrong — religious and non-religious alike — are conclusions about what is real and important in life. For everyone, they serve as a basis for their action in the world.

7. Religious freedom means people are entitled to live out their beliefs in the way they serve the rest of the community

Coming together around a common purpose and shared beliefs to help those in need is one of the main ways in which religious communities encourage participation in society and work to build up a sense of solidarity. Religious freedom protects not only the right of people to live out their beliefs in co-operation with others who share their faith, but also the right to establish and operate services for the wider community that are faithful to the beliefs which inspired them, and which are reflected in their work.

8. Religious freedom is not a claim for special treatment

It is a basic fairness for people to be able to put their beliefs into practice and not to be forced to act against them. Religious freedom protects this basic fairness. It is not a claim for a special privilege or an exemption for religious communities from laws which apply to everyone else, and describing it in these terms is misleading. Religious freedom is a fundamental right which ensures there is a space for religious communities to live out their beliefs, while also respecting the dignity and freedom of other people.

9. Religious freedom reinforces other fundamental rights

Religious freedom is part of a larger whole. It does not sit in isolation but is an integrated and essential part of human rights. Because these rights protect the different things we need to make a full life possible, they have to go together and they should not be placed in opposition to each other. Freedom of religion both depends on respect for rights such as freedom of conscience, freedom of thought, freedom of expression, and freedom of assembly, and supports and reinforces them in turn. Placing religious freedom in doubt places these other rights in doubt as well.

10. Religious freedom makes democratic societies stronger

Religious freedom protects not only the right of individuals and religious communities to fully participate in the life of a democratic society, but also the contribution they make to building it up. Because religious freedom and related protections such as conscientious objection protect people from being compelled to co-operate with activities which they hold, as a matter of conviction, to be wrong, they also help to encourage people to speak out against injustice and evil when no one else will. Good societies need these voices.

Conclusion

Speaking about religious freedom in 2015, Pope Francis highlighted how treasuring their traditions in a spirit which extends justice and mercy to all is part of the contribution religious communities can make to fostering hope and friendship in the societies to which they belong. Hope and friendship sometimes seem to be in short supply today, both in public debate and our life in common. This is another reason why a deeper appreciation of religious freedom is needed, and why the efforts of some to erode it must be resisted.

> In a world where various forms of modern tyranny seek to suppress religious freedom, or ... try to reduce it to a subculture without right to a voice in the public square, or to use religion as a pretext for hatred and brutality, it is imperative that the followers of the various religious traditions join their voices in calling for peace, tolerance and respect for the dignity and the rights of others.[65]

Working for "peace, tolerance and respect for the dignity and the rights of others" might be described as the vocation of religious freedom today. Pluralist democratic societies like Australia need people who live out this vocation. A renewed commitment to religious freedom, approached generously, will help to ensure that this remains possible.

Acknowledgments

This essay has been some time in the preparation and we are indebted to a large number of people who have reviewed drafts and provided comments at different stages during the process.

We are particularly grateful to those who were able to take part in two round-table discussions on the draft paper in the latter half of 2017. It was an enormous help to be able to draw on the expertise of some eminent specialists in this area, including Professor Neil Foster (University of Newcastle), the Rev. Peter Kurti (Centre for Independent Studies), Rocco Mimmo (Ambrose Centre for Religious Liberty), Professor Patrick Parkinson (University of Sydney), Professor Margaret Somerville and Professor Keith Thompson (both from the University of Notre Dame Australia).

It was also an immense assistance to consider a range of perspectives and insights on different points, including those provided by Sr Elizabeth Delaney SGS (National Council of Churches in Australia), Monica Doumat (Catholic Archdiocese of Sydney), Michael Cooney (Australian Catholic Media Council), Professor Gawaine Powell Davies (Buddhist Council of NSW), Peter Wertheim (Executive Council of Australian Jewry), Karin Clark and Dr Pablo Jiménez.

A special debt of gratitude is owed to Jeremy Stuparich at the Australian Catholic Bishops Conference for organising the round-table discussions and for his comments and suggestions. Special thanks also to Debra Vermeer for reviewing the draft and to Dr Robert Dixon from the Pastoral Research Office for his advice on census and survey data and some other points.

We are especially grateful to our colleagues at Australian

Catholic University who were able to comment on drafts and take part in the discussions, including Samantha Dunnicliff, Damien Freeman, Ashley Midalia, Professor Hayden Ramsay, Professor Catherine Renshaw, and Dr Nigel Zimmermann.

To all those who provided comments and suggestions on these essays, our heartfelt thanks. As always, any errors, oversights or bungles in the final product are the responsibility of the authors alone.

Protecting Religious Freedom

Greg Craven

As the vice-chancellor of a Catholic university, I regard protection of religious freedom as a fundamental moral imperative. Authority for this conviction may be found in *Dignitatis humanae*, the Second Vatican Council's Declaration on Religious Freedom, which was promulgated by Pope Paul VI in 1965. Two particular aspects of this fundamental imperative are highlighted in *Dignitatis humanae*:

- First, governments must protect the freedom of each person to seek the truth and to live out their convictions in private and public: To prevent people from bringing their deepest convictions into public life because they are religious convictions or draw on religious understandings is profoundly undemocratic.
- Secondly, while the separation of church and state rightly limits the role of religion in government, religious freedom similarly limits the government from imposing its own agenda or any particular ideology on religious communities.[1]

As a professor of constitutional law and former Crown Counsel in Victoria, I am motivated to contribute to this discussion not only by a shared commitment to the fundamental imperative of religious freedom, but also by a conviction that the legislative means by which we seek to achieve this important end may have serious consequences for the judiciary and its relationship with the democratically accountable legislature.

For both of these reasons, I have come to the conclusion that ensuring religious communities can enjoy a fair go in Australia requires us to change the way in which freedom of religion is protected. This essay sets out four areas in which we need to change the law, and the kind of changes that could be implemented in each, if we are to guarantee that all Australians continue to have a fair go.

What is the human right to freedom of religion?

Any discussion of protection of the human right to freedom of religion requires the clarification of four preliminary matters:

- the meaning of *religion* according to Australian law;
- the significance of *freedom of religion* for adherents of religion;
- the designation of such freedom of religion *as a human right*; and
- the relationship between freedom of religion and associated human rights.

What is 'religion'?

There are many ways in which we can try to unpack the meaning of religion, but, for present purposes, what matters is the law's understanding of what "religion" means. The High Court has wrestled with this challenge on several occasions. Early on, Sir John Latham held, "It would be difficult, if not impossible, to devise a definition of religion which would satisfy the adherents of all the many and various religions which exist, or have existed in the world."[2] That said, the Court has subsequently identified indicia of religion. Sir Anthony Mason and Sir Gerard Brennan held that:

> for the purposes of the law, the criteria of religion are twofold: first, belief in a supernatural Being, Thing or Principle; and second, the acceptance of canons of conduct in order to give effect to that belief, though canons of conduct which offend against the ordinary laws are outside the area of any immunity, privilege or right conferred on the grounds of religion.[3]

In the same case, Sir Ronald Wilson and Sir William Deane identified five indicia of religion:

> One of the most important indicia of 'a religion' is that the particular collection of ideas and/or practices involves belief in the supernatural, that is to say, belief that reality extends beyond that which is capable of perception by the senses. If that be absent, it is unlikely that one has a 'religion'. Another is that the ideas relate to things supernatural. A third is that the ideas are accepted by adherents as requiring or encouraging them to observe particular standards or codes of conduct or to participate in specific practices having supernatural significance. A fourth is that, however loosely knit and varying in beliefs and practices adherents may be, they constitute an identifiable group or identifiable groups. A fifth, and perhaps more controversial, indicium ... is that the adherents themselves see the collection of ideas and/or practices as constituting a religion.[4]

The Australian Law Reform Commission is satisfied that these definitions largely capture what matters about religion for the law's purposes.[5] Furthermore, the law's approach is probably acceptable to both religious and non-religious people in Australia today.

Some of the increasing number of Australians who have no contact with religion of any kind have no sympathy for it either. As a consequence, religion for them might seem to be little more than a set of assertions that are not substantiated by science. This trivialisation of religion easily leads to a trivialisation of religious freedom. From religious adherents' perspective, religion is a shared experience of the transcendent that has ethical implications not only for the life of the individual, but for a community's shared form of life. Professor Scruton captures the sociological dimension of this in his book about the Church of England:

> we need to recognise that religion is not simply a matter of believing a few abstract metaphysical propositions that stand shaking and vulnerable before the advance of modern science. Religion is a way of life, involving customs and attachments by which we live. It is both a faith and a form of membership, in which the destiny of the individual is bound up with that of a community. And it is a way in which the ordinary, the everyday and the unsurprising are rescued from the flow of time and re-made as sacrosanct. A religion has its accumulations of dogma; but dogmas make no real sense when detached from the community that adheres to them, being not neutral statements of fact but collective bids for salvation.[6]

When trying to explain the social significance of religious forms of life for a secular society, the British philosopher and politician, Jesse Norman MP, offers the following reflections on the findings of contemporary sociology:

> It appears, then, that sacred custom and ritual play a crucial role in the longevity and success of religious communities. But it is also striking that the emphasis from this emerging picture is less on revelation than on religions and moral communities as institutions. What matters is that humans as social animals should be able to develop among themselves habits, standards, practices, rules and moral codes to act as binding agents, which endow the world with value and so inhibit Durkheimian anomie and the adverse effects of too much individualism. Of course, this will hardly satisfy those of any religion who insist on the centrality of revelation, access to divine law and the

truth of God's word. But it is where the evidence presently lies about the sources of human well-being.[7]

So it is important that, when we turn our minds to protecting freedom of religion, what we are seeking to protect is not only the right to adopt and follow a particular religious revelation and the systems of belief developed from it, but shared forms of life that endow the world with value and which re-make the ordinary and everyday as sacrosanct for members of religious communities formed around them.

This sense of meaning and belonging also frequently bears fruit in charity and service work for the wider community, which contribute significantly to making Australia a decent society.

Freedom of religion: Giving religious Australians a fair go

If religious adherents are to continue to enjoy a fair go in Australia, the law needs to ensure that they remain free to adhere to their religious faith in at least four contexts:

- belief, worship and assembly;
- teaching and preaching;
- maintaining institutions for religious worship, education and other social services; and
- living out their convictions in the public square.

Freedom to believe, worship and assemble

Few people would dispute that freedom of religion requires that adherents of a religion should be free to hold the convictions of their faith; that they should be free to worship in whatever manner is prescribed by that religion's beliefs, and that they should be free to assemble with fellow adherents for the purpose of such worship.

That all Australians are entitled to freedom of belief, freedom of worship, and freedom of assembly is probably not contentious. Guaranteeing such freedoms does not, however, guarantee freedom of religion. Giving religious adherents a fair go in Australia requires more than that.

Freedom to teach and preach

If any religion is to flourish, the adherents of that religion need to be able to nurture their religious community by teaching co-religionists about their shared religious beliefs, as well as being free to share their convictions with the wider public.

Such religious education may occur in places of worship as part of an act of worship. It might also occur within an educational context, either in institutions established by adherents of a particular religion for their own education about their shared religious beliefs, or within other educational institutions that are not owned or controlled by the religious adherents, such as special religious instruction classes in state schools.

It follows that if religious adherents in Australia are to have a fair go, they need to be free to teach and preach their religious beliefs to other members of their religion and to their children, and to invite others to join them. For many religious traditions, the teaching and sharing of their religious beliefs is not limited to the verbal or written word, or by catechetical instruction to be reasoned out and critically understood through intellectual discovery.

In fact, an abundance of teaching and preaching is conducted through the display and sharing of image, symbol, ritual, and song. For example, the display of the crucifix on a Catholic school, or the cross upon the clothing or jewelry of a Christian lay person, or the image of Mary and the Infant Jesus on the living room wall or at the workstation of a valued employee — these are practices not of the clergy but of ordinary Christians, and their expression both in public and private contexts needs to be recognised and protected for what it is: an inoffensive declaration of faith that is centuries old.

Freedom to maintain institutions for religious worship, education and other social services

The adherents of a religious tradition manifest the values of their tradition in many ways, including through the institutions of their tradition. Institutions consist of people, but are distinct from the people who comprise them.

As Jesse Norman writes, "individually, good habits become internalised into virtues; collectively, they create institutions".[8] When people become members of institutions, the bond of membership is all about feelings of affection, identity and interest. People's values are formed through the institutions to which they belong, but it is a two-way street: people also give expression to their values through their membership of institutions.

Adherents of a particular religion will come together to form religious institutions for a range of different purposes. Central among these purposes are worship, education, alleviation of poverty, burial of the dead, and provision of healthcare, childcare and aged care, which reflect their religious convictions and the habits of service which arise from them.

It is true that some of these religious institutions might have the hallmarks of service providers. It is vital to understand, however, that as religious institutions, they are first and foremost a manifestation of the shared values of the members of that institution. Religious adherents come together to provide certain services because they believe that doing so is a manifestation of their shared religious beliefs and that this is required by them.

Accordingly, religious adherents need to be able to ensure that the people who deliver these services appreciate the shared values that give rise to the commitment to provide the services and are willing to support them, lest the whole purpose of the institution be lost and the institution—as a manifestation of shared values — collapse.

It follows that, if religious adherents are to get a fair go in Australia, they need to be free to maintain their institutions by ensuring that those employed by their institutions, and those who use the premises and other property of the institutions are sympathetic to the shared values that the institutions have been established to manifest.

Freedom to live out convictions in the public square

From the perspective of religious adherents, their religion is a shared form of life, anchored in a tradition whose values are manifest in the institutions of the tradition. This shared form of life gives rise to obligations, which adherents choose to make their own, about how their faith should be lived out in practice; obligations that cannot always be discharged within the private domain. Religious obligations can extend to all aspects of an adherent's life, including activities in the public square.

Such religious obligations might compel the adherent to refrain from doing things that are contrary to the beliefs of the adherent's religious tradition, or to say and do such things as the beliefs of the adherent's religious tradition demand, even if so doing is contrary to the beliefs of the majority of the society in which the adherent lives, or even regarded as "offensive" by some others living within the society but outside that religious tradition.

This presents what is perhaps the most fundamental challenge for religious freedom, and an opportunity for us, as Australians: to display a mature appreciation of how fundamental differences can be accommodated and respected. If our society is to provide for a fair go, it must make space for those who adhere to some minority form of life to adhere to the range of obligations they accept as a member of their religious tradition. The obligations of different religions take different forms, and the challenge for a secular society is to ensure that adherents of different religions are free to adhere to their different kinds of obligations within the public square, subject to respect for the law and the rights of others.

Making space for different kinds of religious obligations within a secular society would include ensuring:

- Catholic doctors and nurses are not required to participate in abortions in public hospitals.
- Muslim women are not prevented from wearing suitably modest attire in public places.
- Jewish parents are not prevented from circumcising their sons on the eighth day after birth.
- Jehovah's Witnesses are not prevented from carrying out their door-knocking missions.
- Salvation Army nursing homes are not required to facilitate voluntary euthanasia.

These are but a few examples. It follows, however, that if religious people in Australia are to get a fair go, they must be free to adhere to such diverse religious obligations, and that people who adhere to minority traditions within Australia must feel that Australian society at large respects their right to do so — however peculiar, backward, or offensive this might seem to others.

Freedom of religion as a human right

To say that you have a legal right to something is to say that you have an entitlement to something and that the law will protect that entitlement. There are, of course, processes through which the law can remove such rights.

To say that you have a human right to something is to say that you have an entitlement to something *in virtue of your being human*. Although the law can take some legal rights away from you, the law cannot strip you of rights that you have in virtue of your being human without purporting to deprive you of your basic humanity.

Our shared humanity, together with the fundamental rights that belong to all of us as human beings, are not gifts of the state. In a decent society, governments should recognise all people as equally human and should recognise and defend the fundamental rights we share. Laws which purport to remove the basic rights of some classes of human beings, or to unjustly limit those rights, in effect deny recognition of the full humanity of these people. Democratic law-making should always avoid this path.

In countries like Australia, a number of discrete aspects of being human come into consideration in protecting or advancing human rights. Four aspects which are particularly important in contemporary Australian public discourse are ethnicity, gender, sexuality and religion. In part, this is from a sense that treating people unfairly because of these attributes is simply wrong, and this is often informed by an appreciation of historical discrimination or injustice. In part, it is also from a shared assumption that, in different ways, these attributes often play an important role in shaping people's understanding of who they are.

Human rights help to ensure that we can access what is required to meet our basic needs and have the opportunity to flourish. Not being subject to detriment, unjust discrimination or persecution because of who we are, or because of our particular attributes, is considered an indispensable precondition for such flourishing in Australia.

Australians have considerable freedom to determine who they are and how they might live, despite the often imperfect and limited nature of human freedom. Some aspects of who we are, however, are not easily changeable, and it is particularly invidious to suffer discrimination or detriment on these grounds.

Freedom of religion is the specific human right which protects the attribute of being religious and the ability of people to live out a religious life. For freedom of religion to be meaningful for adherents of any religion, it will have to guarantee freedom to believe, worship and assemble; freedom to preach and teach; freedom to maintain religious institutions for worship, education and provision of social services; and freedom to live out one's convictions in the public square.

The relationship between freedom of religion and associated human rights

Perhaps the most influential statement of freedom of religion is to be found in Article 18 of the *International Covenant on Civil and Political Rights*.[9] Three important distinctions may be observed in that Article's language:

- religion v belief;
- holding a belief v manifesting a belief;
- manifesting a belief individually v manifesting a belief in community with others.

Article 18 seeks to capture some features of religion and belief which are entitled to similar protection. Whilst non-religious beliefs are worthy of protection, one cannot simply treat them as a non-religious version of religion when it comes to protection of freedom of religion. Religion does include beliefs, but, as Professor Scruton and Dr Norman have explained, there is much more to religion than a catalogue of the beliefs of a religion.

Although it is correct to say that one can hold a belief, and in this sense one can hold a religious belief, one cannot hold a religion. Whereas a belief, be it religious or non-religious, can be held, a religion needs to be *manifested*: simply holding the beliefs of a religion without being able to manifest them through the way one lives one's life does not capture what matters about *religion*, even if it does capture what matters about *religious belief*. Religion is as much a matter of how one lives as it is a matter of what one believes.

The communal expression and manifestation of belief is an essential part of religion. While non-religious belief can also be manifested, holding a non-religious belief need not be communal and need not be manifested to be held.[10] So, whilst individuals should be free to hold their own beliefs, be they religious or non-religious beliefs, freedom of religion is not only a matter of protecting the right for an individual to hold his or her own beliefs. Critically, freedom of religion is also about a religious community being able to manifest its shared form of life.

Religion and belief differ more than the language of the ICCPR suggests: having a religion is a matter of being part of something greater than myself, whereas my having a belief is a matter of my entertaining a proposition or state that is practically unavoidable, and which need not reference belonging, continuity or morality, in the way that religion does. Thus, whilst much of what matters about protecting freedom of religion will also matter for freedom of (non-religious) belief, freedom of religion presents additional challenges. Although the ICCPR regards the right to *hold* a religion or belief as being absolute, the right to *manifest* a religion or belief is not regarded as absolute. So, whereas freedom of belief is unqualified, freedom of religion is necessarily qualified. Thus, the challenge for working out how to protect freedom of religion lies in working out how the qualifications should operate. There is no equivalent challenge for freedom of belief, which is unqualified. This essay is concerned specifically with freedom of religion in the sense of the right for members of religious communities to manifest their religious beliefs, individually as well as through their shared form of life, and the ways in which the state is justified in qualifying that right.

The intersection between freedom of religion and other human rights

When the High Court attended to the interpretation of the religious freedom protection in section 116 of the Constitution, the Chief Justice, Sir John Latham, turned to the writing of JS Mill for guidance:

> John Stuart Mill in his *Essay on Liberty* critically examines the idea of liberty, and his discussion of the subject is widely accepted as a weighty exposition of principle. The author had to make the distinction which is often made in words between liberty and licence, but which it is sometimes very difficult to apply in practice. He recognized that liberty did not mean the licence of individuals to do just what they pleased, because such liberty would mean the absence of law and of order, and ultimately the destruction of liberty. He expressed his opinion as to the limits of liberty when he said: 'The sole end for which mankind are warranted, individually or collectively, in interfering with the liberty of action of any of their number, is self-protection'.
>
> It may be going too far to say that self-protection is 'the sole end' which justifies any governmental action. But I think it must be conceded that the protection of any form of liberty as a social right within a society necessarily involves the continued existence of that society as a society. Otherwise the protection of liberty would be meaningless and ineffective.[11]

I share the Chief Justice's reservations about Mill's claim that self-protection is "the sole end" justifying limits on freedom. Nevertheless, Mill's harm principle would now be widely accepted throughout most sections of Australian society: that is, the state should not interfere with a citizen's liberty unless such is necessary to protect some other citizen's liberty. The question is what constitutes "self-protection" in modern Australia? In terms of self-protection as a defence in criminal law, we have a fairly well-understood sense of what is at stake. When it comes to giving all Australians a fair go, we mean more than just ensuring that their physical person is safe from violation. We mean that everyone should be able to protect that which is at the core of themselves.

What is it that is at the core of ourselves, and which can only be taken away from us on pain of depriving us of our sense of ourselves?

There are at least three ways of answering the question:

- What is at the core of myself is what I cannot change about myself.
- What is at the core of myself is that which is constitutive of who I am.
- What is at the core of myself is that which I am prepared to choose to die or go to prison for.

I appreciate that the four attributes I highlighted earlier — ethnicity, gender, sexuality, and religion — strongly resonate with one or other of these questions for many of my fellow citizens in contemporary Australia and their own sense of who they are.

Aboriginal and Torres Strait Islander people will often speak of the sense in which their ethnicity is so central to their understanding of themselves, and I am struck by the fact that, although my Irish ethnicity might be as significant for my understanding of myself, I have never suffered discrimination on account of it in Australia, in the way that they have, although my forebears might well have known something approaching it at the hands of the English. Whether or not "race-talk" is socially constructed, ethnicity has a powerful impact on the way people understand themselves.[12]

So we need to ensure that people feel their ethnicity, and the contribution it makes to their sense of themselves, is respected, rather than becoming a basis for discrimination.

Gender is also central to many a person's understanding of herself or himself. Whilst feminists disagree about much in their analysis of the problems that sex discrimination law seeks to address, Catherine MacKinnon articulates the problem that it seeks to address as one of seeking to deliver women "a chance at productive lives of reasonable physical security, self-expression, individuation, and minimal respect and dignity" which they "are socially prevented from having on the basis of a condition of birth".[13] The Catholic Church has long been clear that the radical equality of all people includes equality of the sexes, even if it fundamentally disagrees with the theoretical constructs employed by many feminists and gender theorists.[14]

The church has also long been clear about the fundamental importance of love, and its sexual expression, for human beings.[15] More recently, queer theory has found an alternative departure point for its theory of sexuality, in Foucault's *History of Sexuality*, and the shifting focus in the mid-1800s from understanding of sexual acts as discrete activities that could be performed by anyone to seeing them as an expression of a singular nature, or the manifestation of an individual's soul.[16] In recent times, as a society, we have become increasingly sensitive to the sense in which sexuality, orientation and desire contribute in complex ways to an individual's sense of self, and, indeed, the ways in which our selves can be violated through sexual abuse. Although the approaches of the church and queer theory are very much at odds with one another in their understanding of sexuality and the distinction between male and female, this profound disagreement is born of a shared appreciation of the significance that love and its sexual expression has for human beings, and the need to make sense of this. We are a long way from any consensus on this topic, but we are in agreement that sexuality, male/female identity, questions of gender collaboration and mutuality, fundamental equality, and a desire for self-expression are fundamental features of any search for a common sense of happiness and well-being.

These are the sorts of things that one cannot change; that are fundamental to one's sense of oneself; and disputes about which have historically led to conflict and death. They are also the sorts of things that we would usually think the law needs to protect if we are to ensure that people can survive not merely as animals, but as human beings. The *Declaration of Principles of Tolerance*, adopted by UNESCO in 1995, captures this in the idea of "tolerance", which it defines as "respect, acceptance and appreciation of the rich diversity of our world's cultures, our forms of expression and *ways of being human*".[17]

Similarly, for many people membership of a religious community contributes profoundly to their sense of themselves in such a fundamental way. It seems to be an inescapable part of being human that we form convictions, either expressly or implicitly, about the true nature and meaning of our existence, and order our lives on the basis of these convictions.

These convictions need not be religious, as discussed above, but once they have been formed and consolidated they become part of who we are and have a powerfully determinative effect on what we do.

What is often misunderstood among non-religious people is that religious identity is not merely a set of convictions made by an individual, but a set of beliefs and practices of whole communities, and each individual believer will feel bound by the religious tradition to which they belong to uphold, honour and give expression to those beliefs. Hence, while acting completely freely and without coercion, a religious believer is committed to holding his or her common religious teaching and faith commitments as fundamentals from which any departure carries serious spiritual repercussions.

Catholics, for example, will understand themselves to be obligated to attend a celebration of the Sunday Eucharist, notwithstanding genuine obstacles such as infirmary, inclement weather or geographical distance, and that willful avoidance will require a spiritual remedy according to the rites of the church. Observant religious adherents do not pick and choose which of their religion's beliefs and convictions they accept. Rather, they will feel bound to believe them as a consistent and comprehensive package, and at times this will require consistent expression of moral convictions that seem at odds with the popular opinions of the culture in which they live and work.

The point is to ensure that such persons are not discriminated against because of a conviction they are bound to follow, and which will feel as unbreakable as any other human attribute such as ethnicity, gender or sexuality; and for the state to avoid placing such persons in a situation of unwarranted pressure, contradiction and self-reduction.

Because of their convictions, many religious people feel

compelled to help those in need, to resist injustice, and to avoid doing what they deeply believe to be wrong. In theory, they could always choose to do something else. Because of their religious convictions, however, there is no other course open to them. Religious freedom — and the separate right to conscientious objection — is another way in which the law recognises that it is unfair for people to suffer a detriment or discrimination because of the convictions which have come to play such a decisive part in their sense of who they are and how they should live.

The enjoyment of a human right can obviously be limited when such enjoyment involves acting in a way that deliberately and intentionally causes serious harm to others. The trickier question involves what we do when one person's human right seems to conflict with another's human right. In a perfect world, there would be no conflict between human rights. Alas we are all too human and ours all too imperfect a world, so we have no choice but to seek to resolve such conflicts.

We need to move towards a situation in which the law finds a better way to balance the different rights which help to ensure that people can enjoy the freedom to live out what is most important to them and their understanding of themselves. Later in this essay, I consider how we might achieve this compromise.

Australian law's current approach to protecting freedom of religion

Although there is no comprehensive protection of freedom of religion in Australia, various measures are to be found scattered across a range of laws.

Common law

The default position of the common law has always been that a person's rights are entitlements to everything that has not been forbidden by parliament or the law. It is notable that, although English law recognised certain privileges of the Church of England, as the established church in England, those parts of the common law were not deemed applicable to the colony of New South Wales, and so were not received into the common law of the colony upon settlement in 1788.

Blackstone famously wrote that "artificial distinctions and refinements", such as "the mode of maintenance for the established clergy" and "the jurisdiction of spiritual courts", did not form part of the "birthright" law of a settled colony.[18] That said, although there was never an established church in colonial Australia, the common law's protection of freedom of religion has never been more than recognition of a right that may be extinguished by ordinary legislation. Thus, the right to freedom of religion is part of the plenary — albeit alienable — freedom of the individual that exists in Australia until it is limited by parliament or the common law.

Australian Constitution

Together with the right to vote (section 41), to trial by jury in limited circumstances (section 80), to non-discrimination based on state residence (section 117), to free trade between the States (section 92), and to acquisition of property by the Commonwealth on just terms (section 51(xxxi)), freedom of religion is one of the few express rights conferred by the Australian Constitution.[19] Section 116 of the Constitution prevents the Commonwealth from establishing any religion, imposing any religious observance, prohibiting the free exercise of any religion, or imposing a religious test for any public office.

The First Amendment to the Constitution of the United States, on which section 116 was modelled, has conferred much greater rights than section 116, which does not prevent the Commonwealth from imposing legal obligations that some people might find morally objectionable on religious grounds. As Sir Samuel Griffith explains in *Krygger v Williams*, "It may be that a law requiring a man to do an act which his religion forbids would be objectionable on moral grounds, but it does not come within the prohibition of sec 116 ...."[20]

It is notable that none of these prohibitions extend to the States, which retain the constitutional right to curtail religious freedom. The consequence is that most legislation dealing with freedom of religion is to be found at the State level, which seems to be consistent with the intentions of the Constitution's draftsmen.

International law

The General Assembly of the United Nations adopted the *Universal Declaration of Human Rights* in 1948,[21] and elaboration of its contents was provided in the *International Covenant on Civil and Political Rights* in 1966.[22] Article 18 of both of these instruments deals with freedom of religion. The *Declaration of All Forms of Intolerance and of Discrimination Based on Religion or Belief* (the *Religion Declaration*)[23] was proclaimed by the General Assembly in 1981, as a non-binding declaration that further elaborates Article 18 of the ICCPR.

Australia signed the ICCPR in 1972 and ratified it in 1980, but has never adopted it into domestic law, and shows little inclination towards doing so in the near future. It is referred to, however, in various statutes in Australia, and has influenced how domestic law courts have interpreted statutes and developed the common law.

Federal legislation

There are at least five federal statutes dealing with freedom of religion in some way:

- *Fair Work Act 2009*: Prohibits an employer from taking adverse action against an employee on the basis of religion (section 351) and prohibits an award from containing a term that discriminates on the basis of religion (section 153).
- *Sex Discrimination Act 1984*: Religious bodies are given exemptions (in limited circumstances) from the Act's prohibitions on discrimination (sections 37 and 38).
- *Age Discrimination Act 2004*: Religious bodies are given exemptions (in limited circumstances) from the Act's prohibitions on discrimination (section 35).
- *Human Rights (Parliamentary Scrutiny) Act 2011*: The Parliamentary Joint Committee on Human Rights is required to examine all Bills for compatibility

with human rights as recognized in Article 18 of the ICCPR, including freedom of religion.

- *Australian Human Rights Commission Act 1986*: The President of AHRC is required to inquire into and attempt to conciliate:

(a) any act that may constitute religious discrimination (section 3);

(b) any act that may be inconsistent with Articles 18 and 26 of the ICCPR (section 11);

(c) any act that might be inconsistent with Article 1 of the *Religion Declaration* (section 47);

(d) complaints of religious discrimination in employment (sections 3 and 31).

State and Territory legislation

Freedom of religion is protected by statutes in three jurisdictions:

- Tasmania: *Constitution Act 1934* (section 46).
- Australian Capital Territory: *Human Rights Act 2004* (section 14).
- Victoria: *Charter of Human Rights and Responsibilities Act 2006* (section 14).

Anti-discrimination laws operate in all States and Territories. In six jurisdictions, this legislation prohibits discrimination on the basis of "religion",[24] whereas in New South Wales the prohibition on discrimination is limited to "ethno-religion",[25] and in South Australia it covers "religious appearance or dress".[26] In each jurisdiction there are exceptions that ensure that discrimination provisions do not apply to religious organisations when adherence to their religious convictions requires them to act in a way that would otherwise be prohibited.[27] In Victoria, this exception extends to individuals as well as organisations.[28]

Furthermore, religious vilification laws prohibit speech that attacks other people on the basis of their religion in Victoria, Tasmania, Queensland and the Australian Capital Territory,[29] and on the basis of their ethno-religious origin in New South Wales.[30] In each jurisdiction, a human rights commission has been established to consider complaints made under the relevant legislation, including complaints of religious discrimination.[31]

Is this adequate protection?

Although Australians have stumbled along fairly comfortably with limited protection for freedom of religion, there is reason to believe that the current provisions are inadequate for Australia moving forward.

One major factor is that the religious composition of Australian society is changing: whereas some level of religious adherence was the norm in the past, increasing numbers of people now claim no religious affiliation.[32] The law needs to respond to this social change in a range of ways, one of which is to recognise that as religious adherence becomes a less prevalent feature in Australian society, Australians who profess religious faith still need to get a fair go, and this requires a different legal framework from that which sufficed in an era when religious adherence was a dominant feature of Australian society. This message comes through in recent public inquiries.

Relevant public reviews and inquiries

The attention of anyone who has been following this issue will, no doubt, have been drawn to at least three important public investigations, in which some of these issues have been considered over the last decade:

- National Human Rights Consultation report.
- Senate Select Committee report on amendment of the *Marriage Act*.
- Joint Standing Committee interim report on religious freedom.

Human Rights Consultation

On 30 September 2009, the National Human Rights Consultation

Committee, chaired by Fr Frank Brennan SJ, delivered its *Report on the National Human Rights Consultation* to the Attorney-General. The conclusion of this extensive consultation was that the Committee recommended that the Commonwealth Parliament enact a human rights statute, which would include the human right to freedom of religion.

This recommendation proved controversial and met with significant opposition. Such opposition crystalised in *Don't Leave Us with the Bill*, a collection edited by Julian Leeser MP (then Executive Director of the Menzies Research Centre) and Ryan Haddrick.[33] This, combined with other factors, led the Australian government not to accept the recommendation, and, as such, Australia remains unique among comparable countries in not having adopted some form of a bill of rights.

Parliamentary interim report on religious freedom

On 30 November 2017, the Human Rights Sub-Committee of the Australian Parliament's Joint Standing Committee on Foreign Affairs, Defence and Trade delivered its interim report, *Legal Foundations of Religious Freedom in Australia*. The purpose was to review developments since the Sub-Committee's last report on this subject in 2000.

Although the Sub-Committee is yet to make any recommendations, its interim report noted that "religious freedom has very little legislative protection and there is a risk of an imbalanced approach to resolving any conflict between the right to freedom of religion or belief and other rights."[34]

Whilst the Sub-Committee noted that the general presumption of the common law is to assume the existence of rights (including that of religious freedom), "evidence to the inquiry suggests that there has been a slow erosion of this general freedom, or a concern that it may be eroded in the future, by the enactment of legislation, including legislation which seeks to uphold other rights but may conflict with religious freedom."[35]

From the Sub-Committee's perspective, the contentious issue is not whether to protect freedom of religion, but how best to protect it:

> There has been general agreement about the need to formally implement the right to freedom of religion or belief, if not the ICCPR in its entirety. ... The Sub-Committee notes the preponderance of evidence from all sides of the issue support the claim that religious freedom should be specifically protected in Commonwealth law, however this is achieved.[36]

There are two aspects to such protection: enshrining the freedom (either through a bill of rights or a stand-alone religious freedom statute), and reforming anti-discrimination law (either by amendment of existing legislation, or the introduction of a new religious discrimination statute).

It is particularly telling that, in 2000, when the Sub-Committee last visited this issue, it considered the Australian Human Rights Commission's 1998 proposal for a religious freedom statute, and concluded that such an enactment was "unnecessary".[37] Seventeen years later, the same Sub-Committee notes that there is "general agreement about the need to formally implement the right to freedom of religion or belief, if not the ICCPR in its entirety."[38]

In relation to anti-discrimination law, the interim report acknowledges that the current system of exemptions is thought to be unsatisfactory both by advocates committed to religious freedom and those not so favourably disposed towards it: "While many believe the existing exemptions are appropriate, some believe they inappropriately favour religious freedom over non-discrimination, while others believe they are inadequate in their protection of religious freedom."[39]

Parliamentary report on Marriage Act *amendments*

On 15 February 2017, the Australian Senate's Select Committee on the Exposure Draft of the Marriage Amendment (Same-Sex Marriage) Bill delivered its *Report into the Commonwealth Government's exposure draft of the Marriage Amendment (Same-Sex Marriage) Bill*.

The Committee's report stated:

> Should legislation be introduced into a Parliament to legalise same-sex marriage, the committee recommends the provision of a more comprehensive indication of potential consequential amendments. This would enable interested parties to more thoroughly examine and consider the effect of a bill, perhaps enabling a Parliament to reach a consensus position on the issue.[40]

Although legislation was subsequently introduced, there was no opportunity for comprehensive examination of consequential changes that might be required. The report noted some specific amendments that might be required. For example:

> Mark Fowler [Director of Neumann & Turnour Lawyers, Brisbane, and Adjunct Professor at University of Notre Dame Australia] raised another possible detriment to religious charities arising from the Bill. Citing the common law doctrine that a charity's purposes must not be contrary to public policy and authority from the United States, New Zealand, Canada and England and Wales he

argued for amendments to the *Charities Act 2013* (Cth) to ensure religious charities with a traditional view of marriage retain their charitable status.[41]

In addition, the report recognised the need for increased protection for freedom of religion:

> Overall the evidence supports the need for current protections for religious freedom to be enhanced. This would most appropriately be achieved through the inclusion of 'religious belief' in federal anti-discrimination law. The idea of a 'no detriment' clause was not canvassed extensively in this inquiry given that it is not proposed by the Exposure Draft. Should a parliament decide to legislate in this area, further examination of the potential form and consequences of such a clause is required before such a concept could be recommended by the Committee.[42]

Recommendations for improving protection of religious freedom

Given the concerns that have been raised in the two most recent reports mentioned above, I believe that there are four areas in which the Australian government should consider improving how the human right to freedom of religion is protected in Australia:

- Two new commissioners for the Australian Human Rights Commission as an immediate priority.
- Temporary legislative reform to address changes to the *Marriage Act* as a short-term priority.
- Overhaul of federal anti-discrimination legislation as a medium-term priority.
- Consideration of how to implement a federal religious freedom statute in the longer term.

New commissioners for AHRC

As explained above, for many Australians, attributes such as ethnicity, gender, sexuality and religion play a critical part in their understanding of themselves and how they live. Helping to ensure that human dignity is protected for everyone, and that people do not suffer discrimination solely because of important attributes, which go to who they are or to their understanding of themselves, is one of the foundations of a good society today. The federal agency that is charged with responsibility for holding the Australian Government and other persons in Australia to account in relation to the protection of human dignity is the AHRC.

The Commission currently monitors issues relating to

ethnicity through the Race Discrimination Commissioner, and issues relating to gender through the Sex Discrimination Commissioner.

The President and the Human Rights Commissioner both have some responsibilities in relation to sexuality and religion. However, these do not currently have dedicated commissioners (although there are dedicated commissioners for Age Discrimination, Disability Discrimination, and Aboriginal and Torres Strait Islander Social Justice and a Children's Commissioner).

The recent debate about same-sex marriage has drawn attention to a number of issues that some Australians face on account of their sexuality and/or their religion. For this reason, it would be timely for the existing commissioners to be supplemented by two new commissioners: a religious freedom commissioner and a sexual diversity commissioner. In this way, each of ethnicity, gender, sexuality and religion would have a dedicated commissioner.

The primary role of the new commissioners would be to inquire into and attempt to conciliate any act or practice that might be construed as discrimination on the basis of religion or sexual identity, orientation or intersex status, and to monitor acts and practices that might be inconsistent with Australia's international obligations, such as those established by Articles 18 and 26 of the ICCPR. In the case of religious freedom, the commissioner's remit would need to cover not only freedom of belief, worship and assembly, but also the freedom to teach and preach, to maintain religious institutions, and to live out one's religious obligations in the public square.

New federal religious freedom statute

The challenge for guaranteeing religious freedom lies not in whether it should be protected, but how. There are two issues here:

- Is religious freedom to be protected as a stand-alone value, or as one of a set of human rights?
- Should this be done through a bill of rights that declares rights and empowers the judiciary to strike down legislation that is incompatible with the rights granted by the statute, or through a charter that recites values, and directs the judiciary to interpret other laws in such a way as they conform with the values of the federal charter?

In both of these respects, I believe the Government would be well advised to consider the counsel of George Williams. On the first point, Professor Williams has written:

> Any move to bring about an Australian Bill of Rights should follow a gradual and incremental path. Certain core rights should be protected before others, and then in legislation, subject to a legislative override, before any constitutional entrenchment ... [this would] maximise the opportunity to create a workable balance between enabling the judiciary to foster the rights of Australians and not vesting misplaced faith in the courts to solve Australia's pressing social, moral and political concerns.[43]

On the second point, Professor Williams has said:

> I do not support anything like the American instrument, which means courts can strike down laws. I favour the UK approach, which means the courts interpret statutes; and so they effectively take direction from parliament that, in applying anti-discrimination and other laws, there

are certain important rights and values that must be taken into account.⁴⁴

While I have serious reservations about the United Kingdom's model which Professor Williams favours, I agree with him that the government should not consider entrenching any human rights in the Constitution; that statutory protection should be incremental (with the focus on protecting freedom of religion before others); and that this should not empower courts to strike down legislation, but merely to interpret it in light of values recited in the religious freedom statute.

I am concerned, however, that there are two sources of difficulty that this approach will confront:

- First, parliament will need to resolve how courts are to use these values when interpreting legislation;
- Secondly, if certain core rights, such as freedom of religion, are to be protected on an equal footing with other fundamental rights, there will need to be a clear constitutional mandate for such legislation.

Secularist interpretation of religious freedom

*Connolly v Director of Public Prosecutions*⁴⁵ is instructive of the difficulty presented by the United Kingdom's approach. In that case, Connolly was convicted under the *Malicious Communications Act 1988* (UK) for sending photographs of aborted fetuses to pharmacists in an effort to dissuade them from stocking the morning-after pill. She claimed that the *Human Rights Act* required the *Malicious Communications Act* to be interpreted in a way that was consistent with her right to freedom of expression and freedom of thought, conscience and religion. Cardinal Pell has written of this case:

In January 2007 the court dismissed this argument, ruling that freedom of thought, conscience and religion is a right which of its nature is likely to cause offence to others and so must be narrowly constructed. The limitations for protecting the rights of others placed on this right, and in this case also on the right to freedom of expression, were given an expansive reading, so that the 'distress and anxiety' caused to those who saw the photos sent by Mrs Connolly was found to be a violation of their rights. For this reason, the court concluded, 'the conviction of Mrs Connolly on the facts of this case was necessary in a democratic society'.[46]

His Eminence concluded, "This case shows what can happen when a charter of rights is interpreted from the premises of a secularist mindset, especially when it is sharpened, as in Europe, by fear of home-grown Islam."[47] This is the nub of the problem if we proceed to implement a religious freedom statute in Australia. We need to develop a framework that will ensure that the right to religious freedom within a secularist society is interpreted in a way that is sensitive to the needs of religious adherents as well as the premises of a secular society.

We cannot look to the United Kingdom for such an interpretative framework, and further work needs to be done to ensure that a religious freedom statute contains guidelines for interpretation of the rights recognised by the statute, in order to ensure that they do not end up being as narrowly constructed as they have been in the United Kingdom.

Constitutional issues

Although the High Court has held that a charter of rights at the State level is valid, *obiter dicta* of the Chief Justice and four other justices in *Momcilovic v The Queen*[48] suggest that a similar charter at the federal level would contravene Chapter III of the Constitution. The advisory role conferred on the judiciary by the Victorian charter appears to be a non-judicial power, which the Constitution stipulates may not be exercised by federal courts. So it is not clear that the Victorian approach could be replicated at the federal level, even if that were desirable.

The Commonwealth Parliament's legislative competence is limited to the powers granted to it by the Constitution. The external affairs power in s 51(xxix) of the Constitution can be used to make a law "reasonably capable of being considered appropriate and adapted to achieving the purpose or object of giving effect to [a] treaty".[49] A religious freedom statute might be enacted for the purpose of implementing Australia's international obligations under Article 18 of the ICCPR. There is a precedent for this in the *Human Rights (Sexual Conduct) Act 1994*, the long title of which is "An Act to implement Australia's international obligations under Article 17 of the International Covenant on Civil and Political Rights". So it is conceivable that the parliament might enact "An Act to implement Australia's international obligations under Article 18 of the ICCPR".

The High Court has, however, expressed different views about whether section 51(xxix) allows parliament to cherry pick a treaty, so as only to incorporate certain of the obligations that Australia accepted under the treaty. As their Honours observed in the *Industrial Relations Case*:

> It would be a tenable proposition that legislation purporting to implement a treaty does not operate upon the subject which is an aspect of external affairs unless the legis-

lation complies with all the obligations assumed under the treaty. That appears to have been the view taken by Evatt and McTiernan JJ in *R v Burgess; Ex parte Henry*. But the *Tasmanian Dam* case and later authorities confirm that this is not an essential requirement of validity.[50]

So, although the Commonwealth Parliament could pass an Act incorporating the entire ICCPR (subject to reservations that it has lodged) into Australian law, it might not so easily rely on the external affairs power to incorporate Article 18 of the ICCPR alone into Australian law. This problem does not occur in the case of laws preventing discrimination on the basis of race or sex, because Australia is a party to treaties dealing with each of these, and in each case a statute was enacted with the intention of fulfilling all the treaty obligations.[51] International obligations aside, it is not obvious that the Commonwealth has another head of power authorising it to make laws with respect to freedom of religion: although section 116 of the Constitution grants a measure of protection for religious freedom, it does not grant the Commonwealth Parliament any legislative power in relation to religious freedom.

Careful attention needs to be given to these issues, and it cannot, in good faith, be said that we have a convincing solution to the problems that arise in relation to them (in the way that we have a convincing solution for dealing with anti-discrimination legislation, as discussed below). Thus, the Australian Government should affirm its commitment to introduce a bill for a religious freedom statute in the longer term. In the medium term the Government needs to identify a satisfactory framework for ensuring the new statutory right to freedom of religion is not read down as it has been in the United Kingdom, and a basis for recognising this right which will survive a potential constitutional challenge in the High Court.

Reform of anti-discrimination legislation

In 2012, the Australian Law Reform Commission considered the idea of a general limitations clause, proposed by Professors Aroney and Parkinson, to replace existing exemptions clauses in anti-discrimination legislation, and recommended this approach in its Freedoms Report. The Commission further recommended consideration of this approach in its submission to the Human Rights Sub-Committee in 2017. It is an approach which I also support.

The general limitations approach would see anti-discrimination law declare that a restriction does not constitute discrimination if it is reasonably appropriate for advancing a human right protected by the ICCPR. The relevant clause, as reproduced in the interim report, is as follows:

> 1. A distinction, exclusion, restriction or condition does not constitute discrimination if:
>
>> a. It is reasonably capable of being considered appropriate and adapted to achieve a legitimate objective;
>
> ...
>
> 2. The protection, advancement or exercise of another human right protected by the *International Covenant on Civil and Political Rights* is a legitimate objective within the meaning of subsection 1(a).[52]

So, for example, because Article 18 of the ICCPR recognises freedom of religion as a human right, a religious organisation could exclude women from holding a certain religious ministry, and this would not constitute discrimination under the *Sex*

Discrimination Act if a court were satisfied that the exclusion was reasonably appropriate for ensuring that religious adherents were adhering properly to their religious obligations.

Such a clause would see potentially competing human rights (such as non-discrimination on the basis of gender and freedom of religion in the above example) put on a level playing field, without one being subordinated or the other being given special treatment.

Legislative changes consequent to changes to the Marriage Act

The *Marriage Act* was amended last year, but there was no opportunity for consideration of consequential legislative amendments, as recommended by the Senate Select Committee.

There is a number of minor legislative amendments that should be made, such as to the *Charities Act*, based on the experience in comparable jurisdictions where similar laws have already been enacted.

These amendments should be treated as short-term measures, to remain in place until laws of general application can be enacted, through reform of anti-discrimination law in the medium term and a religious freedom statute in the longer term. Once the new anti-discrimination and religious freedom legislation is in place, the temporary amendments, such as to the *Charities Act*, would be otiose and could be repealed, as these matters would then be covered by the new laws of general application.

Conclusion

I believe that the recommendations listed above will make for the best chance of success in ensuring that all religious people — along with everyone else — get a fair go in Australia. All Australians of goodwill should appreciate that it is fair and reasonable to appoint new sexuality and religious freedom commissioners; to reform discrimination law so as to remove the need for religious exemptions; to investigate possibilities for recognising freedom of religion in a federal statute in the longer term; and to introduce some short-term provisions to address uncertainties arising from the recent changes to the *Marriage Act*, until the longer-term solution is identified. This has the potential to alleviate the anxieties of religious communities and individual believers, based on a reasonable and fair effort to treat all Australians equally.

It may not be in our day that Isaiah's prophecy shall come to pass and "the wolf also shall dwell with the lamb, and the leopard shall lie down with the kid; and the calf and the young lion and the fatling together; and a little child shall lead them" (Isaiah 11:6). It is not, however, beyond federal law to lead us to a point at which the human right to freedom of religion dwells peacefully with anti-discrimination law and with protection of other human rights. We must now all work together to make such fair and reasonable reform happen speedily.

Endnotes

Nine Questions about Religious Freedom

1 Francis, Apostolic Exhortation *Evangelii gaudium* (24 November 2013), §255.

2 World Values Survey (www.worldvaluessurvey.org), Wave 3 (1994-98) & Wave 6 (2010-14). In Australia, the Wave 3 survey was carried out in 1995 and the Wave 6 survey in 2012. Sample sizes for Australia were 2,048 and 1,477 respectively. The percentages for those reporting that religion is important in their lives combine both those who said religion was "very important" and those who said it was "rather important".

3 Australian Bureau of Statistics, *Census of Population and Housing: Reflecting Australia – Stories from the Census 2016* (Cat. no. 2071.0). Some detailed numbers have been extracted from the ABS's TableBuilder datasets (http://www.abs.gov.au/websitedbs/censushome.nsf/home/tablebuilder). A census is conducted every five years in Australia, but comparing the 2016 results to those ten years earlier (rather than to the 2011 census) helps to highlight more clearly the changing religious composition of the country.

4 *Ibid*. This is partly reflected in the high level figures for "no religion" in the 2016 Census, which includes "Secular Beliefs and Other Spiritual Beliefs". See *Census of Population and Housing: Census Dictionary 2016* (Cat. no. 2901.0).

5 *Ibid*. Interestingly, these changes in the percentage of the population affiliated with each denomination make it appear as if Catholics had a bigger fall over this period than the Uniting Church. While the shares have changed, however, when the changes are considered in terms of the number of people affiliated with each denomination, Catholics increased by 3.2 per cent and Uniting Church members decreased by 23.4 per cent (with Anglicans decreasing by 16.6 per cent). We are grateful to Dr Robert Dixon for this observation.

6 Pew Research Center, *The Changing Global Religious Landscape*, 5 April 2017. Global population as a whole is projected to increase by 32 per cent by 2060, and although the numbers of those who are religiously unaffiliated will increase, their share of global population will fall, primarily because of significantly lower birth rates compared to religious populations. The report observes: "By 2055 to 2060, just 9 per cent of all babies will be born to religiously unaffiliated women, while more than seven-in-ten will be born to either Muslims (36 per cent) or Christians (35 per cent)". Deaths are also projected to exceed births for the religiously unaffiliated ("natural decrease") and all other religious groups, except Christians and Muslims, during this time.

7 This is extensively detailed in reports such as: Aid to the Church, *Religious Freedom in the World: 2016 Report*; US Department of State, *International Religious Freedom Report for 2015*; and Pew Research Centre, "Global Restrictions on Religion Rise Modestly in 2015, Reversing Downward Trend", 11 April 2017.

8 See for example the cases recorded in Observatory on Intolerance and Discrimination Against Christians in Europe, *2015 Report*.

9 Some of the text in this section is taken or adapted from the submission of the Catholic Archdiocese of Sydney to the Australian Human Rights Commission inquiry on *Freedom of Religion and Belief in the 21st Century* (March 2009).

10 See Article 18 (4) of the *International Covenant on Civil and Political Rights* 999UNTS 171(1966), set out in footnote 39 below.

11 Second Vatican Council, Declaration on Religious Freedom *Dignitatis humanae* (7 September 1965), §10.

12 John Paul II, Encyclical Letter *Redemptoris missio* (7 December 1990), §39.

13 Cf. John Paul II, Encyclical Letter *Redemptor hominis* (4 March 1979), §12.

14 On the common good, see the *Compendium of the Social Doctrine of the Catholic Church* (2004), §§164-66: "The principle of the

common good ... stems from the dignity, unity and equality of all people". It means "the sum total of social conditions which allow people, either as groups or as individuals, to reach their fulfilment more fully and more easily". It is not simply the sum total of the goods of a society, let alone the greatest good of the greatest number, but an indivisible life in common which belongs to everyone and to each person, which fosters "the good of all people and of the whole person" through co-operation and solidarity. Although what it requires specifically will depend on social conditions in any given time and place, the common good is always connected to respecting and promoting the dignity and rights of the person. In the modern world it comprises (among other things) a commitment to peace, effective government and the rule of law, "the protection of the environment, and the provision of essential services to all, some of which are at the same time human rights: food, housing, work, education and access to culture, transportation, basic health care, the freedom of communication and expression, and the protection of religious freedom".

15 Some of the text in this section and in the following section is taken or adapted from the submission of the Catholic Archdiocese of Sydney to the Australian Human Rights Commission inquiry on *Freedom of Religion and Belief in the 21st Century* (March 2009).

16 St Vincent de Paul Society NSW, *Moving Forward: Annual Report 2016-17*, 7 & 43. It is interesting to note that in 2011-12 the number of local conferences was 424, and the number of members was 5,178, compared to 4,282 in 2016-17. The number of volunteers in 2011-12 was approximately the same as in 2016-17 (14,416 compared to 14,499), reaching higher numbers each year in between.

17 St Vincent de Paul Society NSW, *Our Society, Our Plan: Strategic Plan 2013-18*, 5.

18 Francis, Address to the Meeting for Religious Liberty with the Hispanic Community and Other Immigrants, Philadelphia (26 September 2015).

19 *Ibid.*

20 Rémi Brague, *The Law of God* (2005). Trans. Lydia G. Cochrane (University of Chicago Press, Chicago: 2007), 130. See also 142, where Brague quotes Accursius' gloss on Gelasius, which provides the epigraph to this book.

21 Pope Benedict XVI, *Jesus of Nazareth: From the Baptism in the Jordan to the Transfiguration.* Trans. Adrian J. Walker (Bloomsbury, London: 2007), 116-20.

22 *Ibid.*, 114 & 118.

23 On which see Michael Burleigh, *Earthly Powers* (Harper Collins, London: 2005); and *Sacred Causes* (Harper Collins, London: 2006).

24 Francis, Philadelphia Address on Religious Liberty.

25 Some of the text of this section is taken or adapted from Frank Brennan SJ, "The Price of Freedom", *Tablet*, 10 November 2012.

26 George Weigel, "The Catholic Journey to Religious Freedom", *National Review Online*, 20 December 2017.

27 On the influence of Catholic social teaching on modern understandings of human rights, see Mary Ann Glendon, "The Influence of Catholic Social Doctrine on Human Rights", *Journal of Catholic Social Thought*, 10:1 (2013), 69-84.

28 John XXIII, Encyclical Letter *Pacem in terris* (11 April 1963), §§9 &14.

29 John Courtney Murray SJ, "This Matter of Religious Freedom", *America*, 9 January 1965. Reprinted in Thomas J. Massaro & Thomas A. Shannon (eds.), *American Catholic Social Teaching*, 2 vols. (Liturgical Press, Collegeville MI: 2002).

30 *Dignitatis humanae,* §2.

31 *Ibid.*

32 *Ibid.,* §3.

33 *Ibid.,* §2.

34 *Ibid.*, §3.

35 *Ibid.*

36 *Ibid.*, §7.

37 *Ibid.*, §1.

38 Some of the text in this section has been taken or adapted from Fr Frank Brennan SJ, "Conscience and Religion, Freedom and Respect, Due Process and Contemporary Politics", paper presented at the "Religious Freedom in an Age of Equality" conference, Melbourne, 23 September 2016.

39 Article 18 of the *International Covenant on Civil and Political Rights* provides for religious freedom as follows:

1. Everyone shall have the right to freedom of thought, conscience and religion. This right shall include freedom to have or to adopt a religion or belief of his choice, and freedom, either individually or in community with others and in public or private, to manifest his religion or belief in worship, observance, practice and teaching.

2. No one shall be subject to coercion which would impair his freedom to have or to adopt a religion or belief of his choice.

3. Freedom to manifest one's religion or beliefs may be subject only to such limitations as are prescribed by law and are necessary to protect public safety, order, health, or morals or the fundamental rights and freedoms of others.

4. The States Parties to the present Covenant undertake to have respect for the liberty of parents and, when applicable, legal guardians to ensure the religious and moral education of their children in conformity with their own convictions.

40 *International Covenant on Civil and Political Rights*, article 4.

41 Edmund Barton, *Constitutional Convention Debates*, Vol III, 1187-88 (www.aph.gov.au).

42 *Church of the New Faith v Commissioner for Pay-roll Tax (Victoria)* (1983) 154 CLR 120 ("*Scientology Case*").

43 *Ibid.*, per Mason ACJ and Brennan J at 136.

44 *Ibid.*, per Wilson and Deane J at 174.

45 Australian Law Reform Commission, *Traditional Rights and Freedoms — Encroachments by Commonwealth Laws*, ALRC Report 129 (2 March 2016) (www.alrc.gov.au), 131.

46 *Ibid.*, 139, quoting a short article by the Australian Human Rights Commission, "Freedom to Believe and the Freedom to Manifest that Belief", nd (www.humanrights.gov.au).

47 United States Conference of Catholic Bishops Ad Hoc Committee for Religious Liberty, "Our First, Most Cherished Liberty: A Statement on Religious Liberty" (March 2012).

48 For an analysis of this phenomenon and the intolerance it generates towards religious faith, particularly the Christian faith, see Mary Eberstadt, *It's Dangerous to Believe: Religious Freedom and its Enemies* (Harper, New York: 2016).

49 See for example, United States Conference of Catholic Bishops, "Discrimination against Catholic adoption services", USCCB Fact Sheet (2017); "Last Catholic adoption agency faces closure after Charity Commission ruling", *The Telegraph*, 19 August 2010; and more generally, Eberstadt, *It's Dangerous to Believe*, Chapter 5.

50 See for example, "Compulsory sex education: Human rights campaigners criticise government over faith school 'get-out clause'", *The Independent*, 2 March 2017. A recent example from Australia is the anti-discrimination complaint brought against Archbishop Julian Porteous, the Catholic Archbishop of Hobart, for distributing the Australian Catholic Bishops Conference pastoral letter on the same-sex marriage debate to Catholic schools, on the grounds that its teaching about marriage and sexuality was offensive and demeaning. See "Catholic bishops called to answer in anti-discrimination test case", *The Australian*, 13 November 2015.

51 See for example the case of Lillian Ladele, discussed (with other matters which formed an appeal to the European Court of Human Rights in 2012) in "Christian discrimination claims heard by

Europe court", *BBC News*, 15 January 2013; and "Lillian Ladele is the real loser in Christian discrimination rulings", *The Guardian*, 17 January 2013. For a Canadian example, see "Commissioner who refused to marry same-sex couple loses appeal", *CBC News*, 23 July 2009; and "Same-sex nuptials can't be refused on religious grounds, Saskatchewan court rules", *The Globe and Mail*, 10 January 2011.

52 A number of examples of workers being demoted or sacked for expressing their support for traditional marriage are provided in Coalition for Marriage (UK), "Punished For Believing In Traditional Marriage: 30 Cases", 9 April 2016. See also the examples summarised and referenced in Eberstadt, *It's Dangerous to Believe*, xii-xiv.

53 *Abortion Law Reform Act 2008* (Vic), s 8.

54 Article 18 of the *United Nations Declaration of Human Rights* UNGA Res 217 A (III) (1948) provides for freedom of conscience (along with freedom of thought and religion) as follows:

> Everyone has the right to freedom of thought, conscience and religion; this right includes freedom to change his religion or belief, and freedom, either alone or in community with others and in public or private, to manifest his religion or belief in teaching, practice, worship and observance.

Article 18 of the *International Covenant on Civil and Political Rights* (cited at footnote 39 above) makes a similar provision.

Section 4.2.3 of the Australian Medical Association's Code of Ethics makes provision for freedom of conscience as follows:

> Recognise your right to refuse to carry out services which you consider to be professionally unethical, against your moral convictions, imposed on you for either administrative reasons or for financial gain or which you consider are not in the best interests of the patient.

It also requires doctors to inform patients of any conscientious objection they may have (Section 2.1.12).

55 Section 7 of Victoria's *Voluntary Assisted Dying Act 2017* recognises the right of a "registered health practitioner" (a term which includes doctors, nurses, pharmacists and psychologists) not to provide or take part in assisted suicide.

56 See for example, "Salvation Army ordered to permit assisted suicide", SWI (Swiss Broadcasting Service), 6 October 2016; and "Diest rest home must pay damages after refusing euthanasia", *Flanders Today*, 1 July 2016. For more information on both cases see: "Swiss Christian nursing home must allow assisted suicide", *The Catholic Herald*, 26 October 2016.

57 See for example, Swedish Human Rights Lawyers, "Swedish Midwives file complaints to the European Court of Human Rights", 14 June 2017 (humanrightslawyers.eu); "Catholic midwives must supervise abortions, Supreme Court decides", *The Telegraph*, 17 December 2014; and "Pro-life health professionals in conflict between conscience and career", *Deseret News*, 17 March 2012.

58 "Consensus Statement on Conscientious Objection in Healthcare" (http://blog.practicalethics.ox.ac.uk/2016/08/consensus-statement-on-conscientious-objection-in-healthcare/), 29 August 2016.

59 Some of the text in this section has been taken or adapted from Fr Frank Brennan SJ, "Conscience and Religion, Freedom and Respect, Due Process and Contemporary Politics", paper presented at the "Religious Freedom in an Age of Equality" conference, Melbourne, 23 September 2016.

60 ALRC, *Traditional Rights and Freedoms*, 159.

61 Cf. Cardinal George Pell, "Protecting our Freedoms", *Sunday Telegraph*, 6 March 2011.

62 Patrick Parkinson & Nicholas Aroney, "Submission on Consolidation of Commonwealth Anti-Discrimination Laws" (January 2012), 3.

63 *Dignitatis humanae*, §6.

64 Walter M. Abbott SJ (gen. ed.), *The Documents of Vatican II*.

Trans. ed. Joseph Gallagher (Guild Press, New York: 1966), *Dignitatis humanae*, §6, note 18. The Declaration and Murray's notes to it from this volume were subsequently republished with a brief introductory essay in *Law and Justice: The Christian Law Review*, 82/83 (1984) 114-36.

65 Francis, Philadelphia Address on Religious Liberty.

Protecting Religious Freedom

1 George Weigel, "The Catholic Journey to Religious Freedom", National Review Online, 20 December 2017.
2 *Adelaide Company of Jehovah's Witnesses Incorporated v The Commonwealth* (1943) 67 CLR 116, per Latham CJ at 123.
3 *Church of the New Faith v Commissioner of Pay-Roll Tax (Victoria)* (1983) 154 CLR 120 ("*Scientology Case*") per Mason ACJ and Brennan J at 136.
4 *Ibid.*, per Wilson and Deane JJ at 174.
5 Australian Law Reform Commission, *Traditional Rights and Freedoms — Encroachments by Commonwealth Laws* (ALRC Report 129), 2 March 2016, 131.
6 Roger Scruton, *Our Church* (Atlantic Books, London: 2012), 6.
7 Jesse Norman, *Edmund Burke* (William Collins, London: 2013), 271.
8 *Ibid.*, 208.
9 "*International Covenant on Civil and Political Rights*" 999 UNTS 171 (1966) (emphasis added):
> Article 18. 1. Everyone shall have the right to freedom of thought, conscience and religion. This right shall include *freedom to have or to adopt a religion or belief* of his choice, and freedom, either *individually or in community with others* and in public or private, to *manifest his religion or belief* in worship, observance, practice and teaching.
>
> 2. No one shall be subject to coercion which would impair his freedom to have or to adopt a religion or belief of his choice.

3. Freedom to manifest one's religion or beliefs may be subject only to such limitations as are prescribed by law and are necessary to protect public safety, order, health, or morals or the fundamental rights and freedoms of others.

4. The States Parties to the present Covenant undertake to have respect for the liberty of parents and, when applicable, legal guardians to ensure the religious and moral education of their children in conformity with their own convictions.

10 Whilst I note that Article 18 of the ICCPR treats "religions" and "beliefs" as each being capable of being "held" and "manifested", I would respectfully suggest that it would be more accurate to speak of "religious beliefs" being held by individuals, and religions being manifested through the lives and actions of religious individuals and religious communities. "Non-religious beliefs" can also be held by individuals, but it is not obvious what the non-religious equivalent of a religion is, such that a non-religious person who holds a non-religious belief can be said to manifest the non-religion (either individually or in community), in the way that a religious person who holds a religious belief can be said to manifest the religion either individually or in community. For there to be such a non-religion, the non-religious belief would have to form part of a non-religious tradition with non-religious institutions that manifests itself through the life of the non-religious individuals and/or the non-religious community.

11 *Adelaide Company of Jehovah's Witnesses Incorporated v The Commonwealth* (1943) 67 CLR 116, per Latham CJ at 131.

12 The idea of "race" has been prevalent in the West at least since the 1600s, and found expression in nineteenth-century theories that claimed humanity could naturally be carved up into "races", and that some races could be shown to be superior to others. Whilst we are still inclined to speak of ethnicities, we now recognise that there is no scientific basis for these ethnicities: they are groups who identify with each other based on common ancestry and shared social, cultural or national experience, language and religion,

and who will often share similarities in physical appearance. So it is legitimate to acknowledge these socially defined categories, which are not scientifically defined categories, although we must also acknowledge the persisting damage that the pseudo-scientific categories of race have caused and — at least historically — ideas of racial superiority which have now been repudiated by most Australians. See P C Taylor, *Race: a philosophical introduction*, 2nd edn (Polity Press, Cambridge: 2013) for a discussion of the persisting significance of race and race-talk.

13 Catharine MacKinnon, *Feminism Unmodified* (Harvard University Press, Cambridge, Ma.: 1987), 32.

14 See §144 of the Pontifical Council for Justice and Peace's *Compendium of the Social Doctrine of the Church*, 2004) for the Catholic Church's teaching on the radical equality of the sexes and §224 of the *Compendium* for the church's repudiation of gender theories as a cultural or social construct.

15 See §223 of the *Compendium* for the church's teaching on love and its sexual expression.

16 See Nikki Sullivan, *A Critical Introduction to Queer Theory* (Edinburgh University Press, Edinburgh: 2003).

17 *Declaration of Principles of Tolerance*, adopted by the General Conference of the United Nations Educational, Scientific and Cultural Organization on 16 November 1995, Article 1 (emphasis added).

18 *Blackstone's Commentaries*, Vol 1, Introduction, section 4. It is interesting to note, however, that it was held in *Scott v Cawsey* (1907) 5 CLR 132 that the *Sunday Observance Act* of 1780 (21 Geo. III, c. 49) continued to apply in Australia in its unmodified form unless amended by state legislation, as this statute was of general application and had been deemed to apply to the circumstances of Australian colonies on the basis of their predominantly Christian composition in *M'Hugh v Robertson* (1885) 11 VLR 410, per Molesworth ACJ at 429. See A C Castles, "The Reception and Status of English Law in Australia", *Adelaide Law Review*, Vol. 2(1), 1963, 1-31.

19 To these might be added the two implied rights to political communication and freedom of association, which the High Court has found to be implied by the text of the Constitution initially in *Australian Capital Television Pty Ltd v The Commonwealth* (1992) 177 CLR 106: see *Lange v Australian Broadcasting Corporation* (1997) 189 CLR 520 and *Tajjour v New South Wales* (2014) 254 CLR 508.

20 (1912) 15 CLR 366, per Griffith CJ at 369.

21 Adopted 10 December 1948, UNGA Res 217 A (III).

22 Opened for signature 19 December 1966 (entered into force 23 March 1976).

23 Adopted 25 November 1981, UNGA A/RES/36/55. Article 2.2 of the *Religion Declaration* states (emphasis added):

> For the purposes of the present Declaration, the expression 'intolerance and discrimination based on religion or belief' means any distinction, *exclusion, restriction or preference based on religion or belief and having as its purpose or as its effect nullification or impairment of the recognition, enjoyment or exercise of human rights and fundamental freedoms on an equal basis.*

24 *Discrimination Act 1991* (ACT), s 7; *Anti-Discrimination Act 1996* (NT), s 19; *Anti-Discrimination Act 1991* (Qld), s 7; *Anti-Discrimination Act 1998* (Tas), s 16; *Equal Opportunity Act 2010* (Vic), s 6; *Equal Opportunity Act 1984* (WA), s 53.

25 *Anti-Discrimination Act 1977*, ss 7 and 4.

26 *Equal Opportunity Act 1984*, s 85T.

27 *Discrimination Act 1991* (ACT), ss 32-33; *Anti-Discrimination Act 1996* (NT), ss37A and 51; *Anti-Discrimination Act 1991* (Qld), Part 4; *Anti-Discrimination Act 1998* (Tas), Part 5; *Equal Opportunity Act 2010* (Vic), Part 4; *Equal Opportunity Act 1984* (WA), s 73; *Equal Opportunity Act 1984* (SA), s 85ZM; *Anti-Discrimination Act 1977* (NSW), s 56.

28 *Equal Opportunity Act 2010*, s 84.

29 *Racial and Religious Tolerance Act 2001* (Vic), s 8; *Anti-Discrimination Act 1991* (Qld), s 124A; *Anti-Discrimination Act 1998* (Tas), s 19; *Discrimination Act 1991* (ACT), s 67A.

30 *Anti-Discrimination Act 1977*, s 20.

31 ACT Human Rights Commission, Anti-Discrimination Board of NSW, Northern Territory Anti-Discrimination Commission, Anti-Discrimination Commission Queensland, South Australian Equal Opportunity Commission, Victorian Equal Opportunity and Human Rights Commission, and Western Australian Equal Opportunity Commission.

32 In the 2016 Census, 30.1 per cent of the population—a little over 7 million people — described themselves as having "no religion", compared to 18 per cent in 2006. Australian Bureau of Statistics, *Census of Population and Housing: Reflecting Australia – Stories from the Census 2016* (Cat. no. 2071.0).

33 Julian Leeser and Ryan Haddick, *Don't Leave Us with the Bill* (Menzies Research Centre, Barton: 2009).

34 Parliament of the Commonwealth of Australia: Joint Standing Committee on Foreign Affairs, Defence and Trade, *Interim Report: Legal Foundations of Religious Freedom in Australia*, (November 2017), 13.

35 *Ibid.*, 49-50.

36 *Ibid.*, 74.

37 *Ibid.*, 72.

38 *Ibid.*, 74.

39 *Ibid.*, 50.

40 Parliament of the Commonwealth of Australia: Senate Select Committee on the Exposure Draft of the Marriage Amendment (Same-Sex Marriage) Bill, *Report into the Commonwealth Government's exposure draft of the Marriage Amendment (Same-Sex Marriage) Bill*, February 2017, 32-33.

41 *Ibid.*, 68.

42 *Ibid.*

43 George Williams, "The Federal Parliament and the Protection of Human Rights", Parliamentary Library Research Paper 20, 1998-99; as cited in the interim report, 72.

44 Joint Standing Committee on Foreign Affairs, Defence and Trade: Human Rights Sub-Committee, *Committee Hansard*, Sydney, 6 June 2017, 6; as cited in the interim report, 70.

45 [2007] EWHC 237 (Admin).

46 George Pell, "Four Fictions: An Argument Against a Charter of Rights" in Leeser and Haddick, *Don't Leave Us with the Bill*, 233-241, 239-240.

47 *Ibid.*, 240.

48 (2011) 245 CLR 1.

49 *Victoria v Commonwealth* (1996) 138 ALR 129 *("Industrial Relations Case")* per Brennan CJ, Toohey, Gaudron, McHugh and Gummow JJ, at 147.

50 *Ibid.*

51 The *Religion Declaration* is not a treaty, and so it cannot be signed, ratified, or incorporated into domestic law.

52 This is an extract of the form in which the Aroney and Parkinson proposal is reproduced in the Sub-Committee's interim report on 85.

www.ingramcontent.com/pod-product-compliance
Lightning Source LLC
Chambersburg PA
CBHW070556160426
43199CB00014B/2530